ROBERT McCOLLEY (Ph.D., University of California at Berkeley), editor of this volume in the Eyewitness Accounts of American History series, is Associate Professor of History at the University of Illinois. He is the author of *Slavery and Jeffersonian Virginia.*

Federalists, Republicans, and

Foreign Entanglements 1789–1815

Edited by
Robert McColley

A SPECTRUM BOOK

PRENTICE-HALL, Inc., *Englewood Cliffs, N. J.*

FOR ALICE ELIZABETH MCCOLLEY

Current Printing (last digit):
10 9 8 7 6 5 4 3 2 1

Prentice-Hall International, Inc. (*London*)

Acknowledgments

My research in the early years of the Republic has been helped in several ways by the Research Board of the Graduate College, University of Illinois. The Library of the University of Illinois continues to provide immense collections and exemplary assistance. Two scholars, Christine Scott and Robert L. Wagner, helped as research assistants on several of the problems illustrated in this book. For material used here and elsewhere there is a growing debt of gratitude to the Manuscripts Division of the Library of Congress. At the end of this book a brief bibliography lists some of the authorities who have made it possible to study early United States history in depth and detail. My thanks to all of these, and to several from the friendly legions of Prentice-Hall: Edgar Thomas, William Oliver, Theodore Ricks, and Robert Fenyo.

Contents

Federalists, Republicans,
and
Foreign Entanglements
1789–1815

Introduction

From George Washington's first inauguration to Andrew Jackson's victory at New Orleans, the greatest political questions that stirred the people of the United States were questions of foreign policy. Of course, there were lively disputes over domestic issues, but even these had foreign implications. For instance, Thomas Jefferson opposed the economic program of Alexander Hamilton because he feared it would deliver the United States back to the British Empire, but he approved the economic nationalism of the Pennsylvania Democratic-Republicans, who were pro-French. The merchants and farmers of New England, who remained the firmest supporters of Hamiltonian Federalism, were more interested in supporting Britain against the subversion and infidelities of France—as they saw them —than they were in a centrally controlled program of economic advancement.

Considering the nation's situation in 1789, foreign policy had to be the paramount problem for the new government. The British army controlled a series of forts well within the northern treaty line of 1783, and the British intended to stay there until the United States should recognize and guarantee a permanent Indian confederation north of the Ohio River. The Spanish were trying something of the same sort with the Creek Indians, insisting that the United States had no right to the land south of the Tennessee River.

The infant settlements in Kentucky and western Pennsylvania could not flourish unless the whole Mississippi should be free and open for their trade and the Indians, both northern and southern,

1

be subdued. The old Continental Congress had been powerless to deal with these difficulties; whether the westerners would remain loyal to the United States depended upon the ability of the new government to do better.

Territorial problems were grave enough, but commercial problems were graver still. The states of the early union traded more with foreigners than they did with each other. Yet by European standards, they had no system of trade and navigation worthy of the name. Britain controlled their foreign trade and rebuffed all their efforts even to discuss a proper treaty defining the rights of each party. Before independence, Americans had prospered in the trade between the British West Indies and the American mainland, but after 1783, the British closed their colonial harbors to all ships but their own—a common practice in the age of mercantilism—and the British merchant marine monopolized this important commerce. British merchant houses once again controlled the tobacco trade of Virginia, as they had in colonial times, placing the planters in their debt and setting tobacco prices—so it seemed to the Virginians—exclusively to their own advantage.

With one great power, France, we enjoyed a relationship of apparent friendliness. Under the treaties of 1778, the United States and France had promised to trade on the fairest terms with one another and had pledged to defend one another when attacked by Britain. But friendly as they were toward the United States, the French never could give up entirely the idea that they might expand their trade and regain their once immense empire in the heart of North America. Later, under the more energetic governments of Revolutionary and Napoleonic France, their ambition added new distractions to American politics.

Crises and wars between the great imperial powers of Europe offered the United States great opportunities to expand both trade and territory by playing the rivals against one another. In pursuit of these opportunities, all the partisans of the early republic were patriots in their way, however obstinate they were in seeing nothing but foreign and wicked designs in their opponents. The furious disputes between high Federalist and pure Democratic-Republican were over the means of exploiting Europe's quarrels to American advantage. Madison and Jefferson were convinced, in the 1790's, that Britain could be forced to concede on all disputed points if only the United States would exert the proper economic pressure and co-operate intelligently with the French. Alexander Hamilton and a large group of northeastern Federalists saw conciliation and friendship with Britain as the fairest way to American greatness. Theirs was a vision of a grand and prosperous Anglo-American trading empire that eventually would control the wealth of two hemispheres. The French Revolution became an issue well after this difference of opinion had been made clear, but the course of the Revolution made the division in America infinitely more bitter.

George Washington, John Adams, and possibly a majority of public men preferred a foreign policy more cautious and independent than either that of Hamilton or that of Madison and Jefferson. The first two presidents certainly pursued the ends of territorial expansion and increased trade but were not so eager to plunge into the powerful currents of international power politics. Under Washington and Adams, the High Federalists and Democratic-Republicans—that is, the more extreme partisans of Britain and France—were, with difficulty, played off against one another, and the nation fought only minor wars. Jefferson and Madison, on the other hand, pursued a much bolder foreign policy and achieved more spectacular results—huge acquisitions of national territory, and a major war.

Our presentation of the documents that follow is not intended to take the place of a sound historical narrative. Its first purpose is to acquaint the student with the ideals, the ambitions, and the fears that motivated the leaders of early America, as expressed in their public and private papers. The second is to suggest the remarkable variety of issues that contributed, in one way or another, to political division. A few documents illustrate French and British attitudes toward the United States as well. For such momentous events as the Louisiana Purchase or the War of 1812, this collection aims to sketch in long-range causes, leaving the full statement of immediate causes to standard histories. Questions that did not cause deep political divisions within the nation are relatively neglected here: Hamiltonians and Jeffersonians both resented the Barbary pirates, the Spanish in Florida, and Indian resistance to United States expansion.

This collection is intended for reading and not as a definitive text of the documents included. Therefore spelling and punctuation have been altered in several places. The literary usages of the period were so much like our own that this editing does very little violence to the originals and may help the reader to concentrate upon content. Of course, no changes have been made in grammar or vocabulary, and any further editorial tampering has been indicated in conventional and unmistakable ways.

Champaign-Urbana
March, 1968

I

The Crisis in British
Relations, 1789–1796

1. A Prologue—Madison to Monroe,
7 August 1785.

This letter demonstrates Madison's early nationalism and
his desire to improve the trade balances of the United States
by a vigorous and discriminatory navigation act. He is here
discussing with Monroe a proposed amendment to the Articles
of Confederation that would give adequate commercial power
to the Federal Government. It was so difficult to secure the
required unanimous adoption of these amendments that none
ever was ratified during the brief life of the Articles. But
under the Constitution of 1787, Madison had ample authority
to create navigation acts. [*Letters and Other Writings of
James Madison,* Congressional Edition (Philadelphia, 1865),
I, 169–70.]

. . . Viewing in the abstract the question whether the power of
regulating trade, to a certain degree at least, ought to be vested in
Congress, it appears to me not to admit of a doubt but that it should
be decided in the affirmative. If it be necessary to regulate trade at
all, it surely is necessary to lodge the power where trade can be
regulated with effect; and experience has confirmed what reason
foresaw, that it can never be so regulated by the States acting in
their separate capacities. They can no more exercise this power
separately than they could separately carry on war, or separately
form treaties of alliance or commerce. The nature of the thing,

therefore, proves the former power, no less than the latter, to be within the reason of the federal Constitution.

Much, indeed, is it to be wished, as I conceive, that no regulations of trade, that is to say, no restrictions [or] imposts whatever, were necessary. A perfect freedom is the system which would be my choice. But before such a system will be eligible, perhaps, for the United States, they must be out of debt; before it will be attainable, all other nations must concur in it. Whilst any one of these imposes on our vessels, seamen, etc., in their ports, clogs from which they exempt their own, we must either retort the distinction, or renounce, not merely a just profit, but our only defense against the danger which may most easily beset us. Are we not at this moment under this very alternative? The policy of Great Britain (to say nothing of other nations) has shut against us the channels without which our trade with her must be a losing one; and she has consequently the triumph, as we have the chagrin, of seeing accomplished her prophetic threats, that our independence should forfeit commercial advantages for which it would not recompense us with any new channels of trade.

What is to be done? Must we remain passive victims to foreign politics, or shall we exert the lawful means which our independence has put into our hands of extorting redress? The very question would be an affront to every citizen who loves his country. What, then, are these means? Retaliating regulations of trade only. How are these to be effectuated? Only by harmony in the measures of the States. How is this harmony to be obtained? Only by an acquiescence of all the States in the opinion of a reasonable majority. If Congress, as they are now constituted, cannot be trusted with the power of digesting and enforcing this opinion, let them be otherwise constituted; let their numbers be increased, let them be chosen oftener, and let their period of service be shortened; or if any better medium than Congress can be proposed by which the wills of the States may be concentered, let it be substituted; or lastly, let no regulation of trade adopted by Congress be in force until it shall have been ratified by a certain proportion of the States. But let us not sacrifice the end to the means; let us not rush on certain ruin in order to avoid a possible danger. . . .

2. No Discrimination Against Britain, 16 and 17 June 1789.

One of the first tasks of the First Congress was to supply the United States with revenue. Mercantile interests warned that coercive restrictions against British trade would paralyze American commerce and defeat, at the outset, the hope of raising revenue. Madison argued that we ought to distinguish between nations having commercial treaties with us (France) and those having no such treaties (Britain). The more cautious mercantile view prevailed, to the disgust of William Maclay, the Senator from western Pennsylvania, who kept the best record we have of the earliest session of the Senate. He colored his views with the honest prejudices of a western republican, deeply suspicious that the Hamiltonians and the title-conscious John Adams were trying to create an American aristocracy. [George W. Harris, ed., *Sketches of Debate in the First Senate of the United States, by William Maclay* (Harrisburg, 1880), pp. 80–81.]

. . . Some observations having called me up this day, I endeavored to comprise all I had to say in as little bounds as possible, by observing that there were two extremes in commercial regulations equally to be avoided. The principle of the navigation act might be carried so far as to exclude all foreigners from our ports. The consequence would be a monopoly in favor of the mercantile interest. The other was an unlimited license in favor of foreigners, the consequence of which would be a monopoly in favor of the cheapest carriers, and, in time, a total dependence on them. Both extremes ought to be avoided, by giving certain indulgences to our own trade and that of our friends, in such degree as will secure them the ascendency without hazarding the expulsion of foreigners from our ports.

. . . The amendments, for which we may thank the influence of this city [New York], for doing away the discrimination between foreigners in and out of treaty with us, have been carried. It was in vain that I gave them every opposition in my power. I laid down a marked difference between impost and tonnage. The former imposition is paid by the consumer of the goods; the latter rests on the owner of the ship, at least in the first instance. That sound policy dictated the principle of encouraging the shipping of our friends; that nations not in treaty would not be considered as the most friendly. I read the fifth article of the commercial treaty with *France,* and denied that we had any power of imposing any tonnage on her shipping, save an equivalent to the one hundred sols on *coasters.* I gave my unequivocal opinion, that a want of discrimination in her favor was contrary to the spirit of the treaty, and expressed fears of her resentment.

Ellsworth answered me; but the most that he said was that *our interest* called for it; and he pledged himself that we would never hear from France about it. But speaking was vain. I never saw the Senate more listless or inattentive, nor more determined.

3. Puritanism and Politics, January, 1792.

Foreign policy questions remained concealed from public view during Washington's first administration, but there were serious behind-the-scenes developments. In 1789, Hamilton met secretly with an unofficial British agent, George Beckwith, to assure him that the United States desired a friendly understanding with Britain. In 1790, Jefferson and Hamilton divided, in the Cabinet, over the question of allowing Britain to move troops through American territory in an expected war against Spain. Gouverneur Morris went to London in 1791 as a semi-official representative of the United States and, much to Hamilton's annoyance, made no progress toward a treaty. Later, when Morris had gone to France as the official Minister, the Democratic-Republicans denounced him for his alleged hostility to the progress of the French Revolution and for his undoubted efforts on behalf of French friends who had become political undesirables. The following speech illuminates not Morris's own fascinating diplomatic career, but rather the character of the Connecticut Federalist, Senator Roger Sherman, who voted against the appointment of Morris as Minister to France. The unbending piety of much of New England was soon to become a big factor in party divisions over foreign policy. [Charles R. King, ed., *The Life and Correspondence of Rufus King* (New York, 1894), I, 420.]

I ought in the first place to observe, that I bear Mr. Morris no ill will—I have personally known him for several years; I have served with him in Congress, and was with him in the Convention of 1787. I have never been borne down by his superior talents, nor have I experienced any mortifications from the manner in which he has treated me in debate. I wish him and all mankind holy and happy. . . .

With regard to his moral character, I consider him an irreligious and profane man—he is no hypocrite and never pretended to have any religion. He makes religion the subject of ridicule and is profane in his conversation. I do not think the public have as much security from such men as from godly and honest men—It is a bad example to promote such characters; and although they may never have betrayed a trust, or exhibited proofs of a want of integrity, and although they may be called men of honor—yet I would not put my trust in them. I am unwilling that the country should put their trust in them, and because they have not already done wrong, I feel no security that they will not do wrong in future. General Arnold was an irreligious and profane character—he was called a man of honor, but I never had any confidence in him, nor did I ever join in promoting him. I remember he sued a man at New Haven for saying he had the foul disease, and it was urged that the jury should give heavy damages, because Arnold was a man of honor and high-minded—but this same Arnold betrayed his trust when he had an opportunity and would have delivered up the Commander-in-Chief and betrayed his country. And the like has happened from other such characters; and I am against their being employed and shall therefore vote against Mr. Morris.

4. The Northwest Boundary Question, Summer, 1792.

In early November, 1791, an ill-assorted American army under General Arthur St. Clair, Governor of the Northwest Territory, started a northward expedition from the banks of the Ohio (near present Cincinnati) to assert American sovereignty over the Indians. But the Indians fell upon St. Clair's troops, slaughtered over half of them, and demolished American pretensions for three more years. As a direct result of St. Clair's defeat, the British renewed their diplomatic efforts to create an Indian satellite state between the United States and Canada. The western citizens of the United States were disgusted by the Indian triumph. Along with the continued failure of the Federal Government to open the Mississippi and with its imposition of a tax on distilled liquors, the Indian crisis brought westerners to the point of rebellion. Meanwhile the militarily weak British governors of Canada, who were dependent upon Frenchmen and Indians of problematic loyalty, tried to make the most of the United States' failure. The following dispatch was sent to London early in the summer of 1792; the captured letter to which it refers, from General Henry Knox, American Secretary of War, to St. Clair, was written on 14 July 1791. [Henry Adams Transcripts: Canada, Colonial Correspondence, 1789–1798. Library of Congress.]

Colonel Alexander McKee to Sir John Johnson, copied and forwarded to the home government:

I have just received by a scout from the Glaize the Secretary of War's instructions to General St. Clair, which shall be copied and sent you by the first conveyance; they were got with much difficulty from George White Eyes, who, I understand, has a great many more papers which I expect Capt. Elliott will bring with him. Burns, who accompanied White Eyes, was examined by the Indians at their councils, and suffered death by the hatchet—the same scout brings account of the advanced posts from Fort Washington being evacuated.

Extracts from General Knox's instructions to General St. Clair:

The post at the Miami village is intended for the purpose of awing and curbing the Indians in that quarter, and as the only preventative of future hostilities.

The establishment of said post is considered as an important object of the campaign, and is to take place in all events.

The force contemplated for the garrisons of the Miami village, and its communications has been from a thousand to twelve hundred noncommissioned officers and privates.

The establishment of a post at the Miami village will probably be regarded by the British officers on the frontiers as a circumstance of jealousy. It may therefore be necessary that you should, at a proper time, make such intimations as may remove all such dispositions. This intimation had better follow than precede the possession of the post, unless circumstances dictate otherwise; as it is not the inclination or interest of the United States to enter into a contest with Great Britain, every measure tending to any discussion or altercation must be prevented.

5. Pitt's Government Declines to Fight for the Indians.

Henry Dundas, British Secretary for Home Affairs, wrote the following letter to Lieutenant Governor Alured Clarke on 15 August 1792, reflecting the success of Hamilton in convincing the British Minister, George Hammond, that American sovereignty in the Northwest was an absolute condition of peace and friendship with Britain. [Henry Adams Transcripts, Library of Congress.]

Sir, . . . From the tenor of the dispatches transmitted here by Mr. Hammond, I am sorry to observe that the proposed interposition of his majesty by his good offices between the American States and the belligerent Indians, is not likely to meet with that favourable reception from the former, which a system so beneficial to all parties justly merits, and which of course will not be brought forward at all unless [there is] a reasonable presumption of its being adopted —On this point, however, you will be more particularly informed by Mr. Hammond and you will take your measures accordingly. . . .

6. A Canadian Officer Spoiling for a Fight, 20 August 1792.

Ultimately, the United States and Britain avoided war in the 1790's because both nations were governed by men who had, respectively, a genuine desire for peace with the other country, founded on at least a measure of respect for it. But many loyal Britons hated the United States, as many Americans hated Britain. The multiplication of such characters, who fed and flourished on one another, ultimately led to the War of 1812. According to the wish of John Graves Simcoe, the efficient and determined military governor of Upper Canada, that war should have come fifteen years sooner. Here he sets forth to Lieutenant Governor Clarke his views on the American people. [Henry Adams Transcripts, Library of Congress.]

Sir, . . . My long and uniform observation on the rulers of the United States has never suffered me to hold but one opinion on the subject of all our attempts at negotiation with them; which is that they mean nothing less than amicable arrangement on the subject of the *posts*, and that they will never consent to any commercial treaty whatsoever, that may be of reciprocal benefit—and, that if Great Britain shall deem it necessary to effectuate either, on fair and equal principles, she can never succeed until Mr. Washington, Jefferson, and Hamilton have lost the direction of the Confederation, and this I believe it will be less difficult to effect, by aiming at once to dissolve the confederacy, than by any other secondary or indirect means. With such a firm and uniform belief I am not in the least surprised to find that Mr. Hammond has no hopes of success in a plan that would secure the present generation, and provide for the happiness of posterity; nor do I in the least wonder that in his conversation, Mr. Hamilton, without entering into any argument should coolly and briefly reply, "That any plan that comprehended anything like cession of territory or right, or the allowance of any other power to interfere in the disputes with the Indians, would be considered by this government as absolutely impracticable and inadmissible," at once showing a predetermined spirit not only to preclude Great Britain from all mediation in behalf of the independent Indian nations, but also not to admit a discussion of her own right to retain the posts. . . .

There is no person perhaps who thinks less of the talents or integrity of General Washington than I do; a laudable attachment to his native country as well as his natural avarice and vanity, two principal ingredients of his character, might account for his anxiety to establish the Capital of the United States near his own Estate, and in Virginia; but I have little doubt but his conduct on these particulars is actuated by cool deliberation and foresight and that the capital in Virginia (its confines), the Indian War and the standing army, all tend to one point, namely the joining the western and southern territories to oppose the increase of power of the eastern (northern) states, whose industrious, domineering, and enterprising spirit added to the superior advantages of climate, will without this balance, in no very distant period absolutely command their present confederates. Should Mr. Washington and his colleagues succeed in their present attempt to colonize on the Ohio, I doubt not but the strictest Act of Navigation throughout the Confederation will take place, to flatter and consolidate the eastern with the southern and western states and that the government of the whole will through Mr. Washington and his colleagues sooner or later center in the hands of the French. . . .

Should Congress adopt a Prince of the House of Brunswick for their future President or King, the happiness of the two nations would be interwoven and united, all jealousies removed and the most durable affection cemented that perhaps ever were formed between two independent nations.

This is an object worthy the attention of Great Britain and which many of the most temperate men of the United States have in contemplation, and which many events, if once systematically begun, may hasten and bring to maturity.

7. The Government of France, Toward the End of 1792, Contemplates a Revolution in Louisiana.

In 1792, the French National Assembly, led by the radical Girondists, declared Louis XVI a traitor, executed him, and proclaimed the French Republic. None of the monarchies of Europe recognized the legitimacy of this new French government, and soon many were at war with it. The United States, itself a revolutionary republic, was the only nation to maintain normal diplomatic relations with the French. After the execution of the King, this policy became the subject of popular divisions, with American Federalists taking a pessimistic view of developments in France, and Democratic-Republicans remaining enthusiastic supporters. Whereas all French governments wished the United States well, they did so in a surprisingly traditional French way. The Democratic-Republicans might well have cooled toward their revolutionary cousins had they realized that almost every succeeding French government between the *ancien régime* and Napoleon would have some sort of scheme for re-establishing the French Empire, or a satellite thereof, in the heart of North America. This anonymous memoir from the French Archives of Foreign Affairs describes one of many projects concocted in the 1790's; it was drawn up with particular reference to the important diplomatic mission of Edmond Charles Genêt to the United States. [Translated from the original French version printed in *Annual Report of the American Historical Association for the Year 1896* (Washington, 1897), I, 945–47, 950–51.]

Properly to view this interesting question, it is necessary entirely to strip it of its marvelous aspects, to see only that which it truly reveals.

To embrace at the same time the immense country which extends from New Mexico to Chile to make revolutions there would be to wish to lose sight of realities, to busy oneself with chimeras. Without doubt these vast possessions will not always remain under the Spanish yoke. But it is not up to us to free them today.

Louisiana promises successes most immediate, most certain, and least expensive. These successes are not infallible, but most probable.

To place the Ministry in a position to judge, I am going to submit in a few words the motives for this enterprise, along with a view of the preparations to make, the means to employ, the expenses, and the political consequences which will result.

I will be brief, because the proofs of the facts that I advance are found in a Memoir of which a copy is attached. It is the fruit of researches that I made during five years. I believed I would be able to engage our former Government to negotiate with Spain the retrocession of Louisiana, but circumstances did not permit them to take it up.

Motives for the Enterprise

1. The importance of making a diversion in Louisiana, of alarming Spain for the possession of her western colonies, and of making her use there a part of her troops to protect New Mexico. Perhaps ten thousand men would not suffice to secure that frontier, when Louisiana shall be free.

2. The disposition of the inhabitants, almost all Frenchmen or Anglo-Americans, sworn enemies of a handful of Spaniards who in truth do not oppress them, but constrain their industry and their trade. The resentment they have conserved against the barbarous manner in which Spain signaled her taking possession.

3. The weakness of the garrisons, which at New Orleans, at Natchez, and in the other forts have stationed altogether fifteen hundred men, commanded in part by French Creoles, and spread over a surface of around six hundred leagues in thirty different posts. New Orleans has only three hundred and fifty—three quarters of them French.

4. The character of the inhabitants, which much resembles that of the Anglo-Americans: they are robust, enterprising, good hunters, and friends of liberty, besides being all armed. Since 1779 they have been making overtures secretly to the French Minister at Philadelphia to engage us to relieve them of the Spanish yoke. News

of the revolution in France has made among them the most lively sensation. There is wanting nothing but the assurance of being protected for them to rise.

5. Nothing more easy than the defense of Louisiana from the sea. Reading in the attached Memoir the detailed description of the mouths of the Mississippi will convince one that it is impossible to take New Orleans against the will of the inhabitants. By land the Louisianians have nothing to fear, and the revolution once accomplished would be impossible to undo.

6. The utility of that revolution would be very great for the number of corsairs who, sailing from the mouths of the Mississippi, could infest all the coasts of the Gulf. . . .

What Should Be Our Conduct with Regard to the United States?

For everyone who knows the politics of the free Americans this question is the most difficult to resolve.

Should we include in our secret the chiefs of that republic, or should we act without their concurrence?

Would the Louisianians want to reunite themselves with France or with the United States?

Is it in the interest of the United States to receive them? Is it even in their interest to aid the independence of Louisiana?

Can we act on the Ohio without compromising the neutrality of the United States?

All these questions, some more embarrassing than others, were engaged at the beginning.

To respond to them one ought not lose from view the following observations.

For ten years the independence of Louisiana would have been considered by the Americans as infinitely desirable, because Americans have always enthusiasm for liberty.

The enjoyment has made them calm; they do not treat liberty as lovers but as husbands; everyone among them calculates and arranges; reflection guides them well, but makes them cold.

I know that the most informed and influential men among them, far from desiring the independence of Louisiana, have not even made vows for the liberty of navigating the Mississippi; here is the reason.

Nature has traced the future revolutions of North America. All the territory of the United States from the sea to the Mississippi is cut from North to South by long chains of mountains, which hold the sources of an infinity of rivers, of which some flow toward the Mississippi and others toward the sea. The eastern part is peopled, the western is almost not. The climates of the two countries offer enough differences that one would find them in the interests of the inhabitants. The ones will direct all their speculations toward New Orleans, which will be their only outlet; the others toward the established towns on the shores of the Atlantic Ocean. . . .

I am told that Congress has recently made demands at Madrid to obtain the free navigation of the Mississippi. But these demands do not prove the interest it places there. They prove only that one could not refuse the demands of Kentucky, which forms today a fifteenth State and which has made of this demand a tacit condition of her joining the confederation.

That liberty of navigation and the independence of Louisiana would lead into that country an immense population at the expense of the United States. By the progressive increase of that population the separation between the Atlantic States and those of the West would be inevitable. The Americans know it and do what is possible to delay the event.

It would seem to me after this that the Minister Genêt could not have too much reserve and circumspection in the execution of this enterprise. . . .

8. The German Society of Philadelphia Drinks to Patriotism, Progress, and France, 16 December 1792.

Not all the Germans of Pennsylvania dedicated themselves to rustic isolation and pietistic religion. A large group of German-Americans were active in public life and, as the following newspaper story shows, fully supported the Democratic-Republican Party. The practice of drinking toasts and then publishing them in the newspapers was a central feature of early United States politics. [*General Advertiser*, Philadelphia, 1 January 1793.]

At a general meeting of the members of the German Society, on the 16th inst. at the Lutheran schoolhouse in this city, the annual election of their officers was held and the following gentlemen were duly chosen.

President, Frederick A. Muhlenberg.

Vice-president, Lewis Farmer.

Treasurer, John Steinmetz. . . .

The business of the day being finished, the members of the society proceeded to Mr. Epple's tavern, and partook of an entertainment provided for the occasion, at which the following toasts were drank:

1. The United States.

2. The President of the United States.

3. The Vice-president of the United States.

4. The State and Government of Pennsylvania.

5. The Commonwealth of France—May its arms and example exterminate tyranny and inequality.

6. The German Societies throughout America.

7. The different societies in the United States for promoting humane and charitable purposes.

8. The Germans in the State of Pennsylvania—may they be sensible of their true interest, and advance their character by a proper conduct.

9. The Rights of Man—may they become the political prayer book of the whole world.

10. May the trumpet of Liberty never cease to sound till all mankind are free.

11. The arts and sciences in America.

12. The commerce of the United States.

13. The plow—may every free man reverence it as the fountain of prosperity to the United States.

14. The unfortunate Lafayette—may Justice acquit, and Liberty reward him.

15. May every freeman in America rally round the standard of equality.

A Volunteer. A Burgoynade to the chief of slaves, the Duke of Brunswick.

After which they parted in the utmost harmony and good humor.

9. Thomas Jefferson Avows His Faith in the Revolution, 3 January 1793.

Not since he was Governor of Virginia, with British armies deranging his state, had Thomas Jefferson suffered such trying circumstances as those he met in the year 1793, his last as Secretary of State. To his growing feud with Alexander Hamilton there soon was added the war between France and Britain, declared by the former in February. The following letter sets forth Jefferson's fundamental attitude toward world politics at the beginning of the year. It was written to edify William Short, Jefferson's protégé, and the chargé d'affaires in Paris. [Paul L. Ford, ed., *The Writings of Thomas Jefferson* (New York, 1892–99), VI, 153–55.]

. . . The tone of your letters had for some time given me pain, on account of the extreme warmth with which they censured the proceedings of the Jacobins of France. I considered that sect as the same with the Republican patriots, and the Feuillants as the Monarchical patriots, well known in the early part of the revolution, and but little distant in their views, both having in object the establishment of a free constitution, and differing only on the question whether their chief executive should be hereditary or not. The Jacobins (as since called) yielded to the Feuillants and tried the experiment of retaining their hereditary executive. The experiment failed completely, and would have brought on the re-establishment of despotism had it been pursued. The Jacobins saw this, and that the expunging that officer was of absolute necessity. And the Nation was with them in opinion, for however they might have been formerly for the constitution framed by the first assembly, they were come over from their hope in it, and were now generally Jacobins. In the struggle which was necessary, many guilty persons fell without the forms of trial, and with them some innocent. These I deplore as much as anybody, and shall deplore some of them to the day of my death. But I deplore them as I should have done had they fallen in battle. It was necessary to use the arm of the people, a machine not quite so blind as balls and bombs, but blind to a certain degree. A few of their cordial friends met at their hands the fate of enemies. But time and truth will rescue and embalm their memories, while their posterity will be enjoying that very liberty for which they would never have hesitated to offer up their lives. The liberty of the whole earth was depending on the issue of the contest, and was ever such a prize won with so little innocent blood? My own affections have been deeply wounded by some of the martyrs to this cause, but rather than it should have failed, I would have seen half the earth desolated. Were there but an Adam and Eve left in every country, and left free, it would be better than as it now is. I have expressed to you my sentiments, because they are really those of 99 in a hundred of our citizens. The universal feasts, and rejoicings which have lately been had on account of the successes of the French showed the genuine effusions of their hearts. You have been wounded by the sufferings of your friends, and have by this circumstance been hurried into a temper of mind which would be extremely disrelished if known to your countrymen. The *reserve of the President of the United States* had never permitted me to discover the light in which he viewed it, and as I was more anxious that you should satisfy him than me, I had still avoided explanations with you on the subject. But your [Despatch Number] 113 induced him to break silence and to notice the extreme acrimony of your expressions. He added that he had been informed the sentiments you expressed *in your conversations* were equally offensive to our allies, and that you should consider yourself as the representative of your country and that what you say might be imputed to your constitu-- ents. He desired me therefore to write to you on this subject. He added that he considered *France as the sheet anchor of this country and its friendship as a first object*. There are in the U.S some characters of opposite principles; some of them are high in office, others possessing great wealth, and all of them hostile to France and fondly looking to England as the staff of their hope. These I named to you on a former occasion. Their prospects have certainly not brightened. Excepting them, this country is entirely republican, friends to the Constitution, anxious to preserve it and to have it administered according to its own republican principles. The little party above mentioned have espoused it only as a steppingstone to monarchy, and have endeavored to approximate it to that in its administration in order to render its final transition more easy. The successes of republicanism in France have given the *coup de grâce* to their prospects, and I hope to their projects. I have developed to you faithfully the sentiments of your country, that you may govern yourself accordingly.

10. The Irrepressible Genêt, 23 May 1793.

Edmond Charles Genêt officially presented himself to the United States government on 17 May 1793, but he already had been in the United States for six weeks. Landing in Charleston, South Carolina, he had immediately begun commissioning privateers to prey upon British commerce and recruiting volunteers for French armies of liberation to march against Florida and Louisiana. Flamboyant and obtuse, he was blamed by Jefferson for the grave setback in Franco-American relations that came in 1793. But as Genêt later remarked in his own defense, his actual deeds were those prescribed in his instructions; it was the policy of Girondist France to convert the United States into a naval base against British shipping, the American merchant fleet into an auxiliary of French trade, and the western and southern territories into bases for attacks on Spanish territory. Jefferson and Madison had regretted Washington's Neutrality Proclamation of 21 April, but only because it gave relief to the British without demanding anything from them in return. The Democratic-Republican leaders had no desire to become cobelligerent with France, and were increasingly horrified at Genêt's efforts in that direction. Horror had not set in, however, when the following proclamation was issued by Genêt. Americans, delighted at the prospective profits to be made in the French colonial trade, failed to anticipate that the British would scarcely relax their blockades for our benefit. [*A Message of the President of the United States to Congress Relative to France and Great Britain, Delivered December 5, 1793, with the Papers Therein Referred to.* Published by Order of the House of Representatives (Philadelphia, 1793), p. 15.]

The Citizen Genêt, Minister plenipotentiary, of the French Republic, to Mr. Jefferson, Secretary of State for the United States.

Sir,   Single, against innumerable hordes of tyrants and slaves, who menace her rising liberty, the French nation would have a right to reclaim the obligations imposed on the United States, by the treaties she has contracted with them, and which she has cemented with her blood; but strong in the greatness of her means, and of the power of her principles not less redoubtable to her enemies than the victorious arm which she opposes to their rage, she comes, in the very time when the emissaries of our common enemies are making useless efforts to neutralize the gratitude, to damp the zeal, to weaken or cloud the view of your fellow citizens; she comes, I say, that generous nation, that faithful friend, to labor still to increase the prosperity and add to the happiness which she is pleased to see them enjoy.

The obstacles raised with intentions hostile to liberty, by the perfidious ministers of despotism—the obstacles whose object was to stop the rapid progress of the commerce of the Americans, and the extension of their principles, exist no more. The French Republic, seeing in them but brothers, has opened to them by the decrees now enclosed, all her ports in the two worlds; has granted them all the favors which her own citizens enjoy in her vast possessions; has invited them to participate [in] the benefits of her navigation, in granting to their vessels the same rights as to her own; and has charged me to propose to your government, to establish in a true family compact, that is in a national compact, the liberal and fraternal basis on which she wishes to see raised the commercial and political system of two people, all whose interests are confounded.

I am invested, sir, with the powers necessary to undertake this important negotiation of which the sad annals of humanity offer no example before the brilliant era at length opening on it.

11. Genêt Tells Jefferson His Duty, 22 June 1793.

As Secretary of State, Thomas Jefferson had the task of instructing Genêt in the rules of American neutrality. Our Treaty of Alliance of 1778 obliged us to receive in our harbors the warships, privateers, and prizes of France, while excluding those of her enemies. But Genêt used the Treaty as license to commission and equip privateers and to recruit Americans to man them; furthermore, he insisted on setting up French courts to judge prizes. Our neutrality could not bear the arming of ships; our sovereignty could not yield to the prize courts. The more Jefferson remonstrated on these themes, the more Genêt replied that the executive government was betraying France, and doing so against the wish of the American people. The following outburst is typical. [Same source as No. 10, pp. 30–31.]

Sir, Discussions are short, when matters are taken upon their true principles. Let us explain ourselves as republicans. Let us not lower ourselves to the level of ancient politics, by diplomatic subtleties. Let us be as frank in our overtures—in our declarations, as our two nations are in their affections; and by this plain and sincere conduct, arrive at the object by the shortest way.

All the reasonings, Sir, contained in the letter, which you did me the honor to write me the 17th of this month, are extremely ingenious; but I do not hesitate to tell you, that they rest on a basis which I cannot admit. You oppose to my complaints, to my just reclamations, upon the footing of right, the private or public opinions of the President of the United States; and this aegis not appearing to you sufficient, you bring forward aphorisms of Vattel, to justify or excuse infractions committed on positive treaties. Sir, this conduct is not like ours. In arriving among you, I have, with candor, said that the French nation, cherishing the interests of the United States more than their own, occupied themselves but on their happiness, in the midst of the surrounding dangers, and instead of pressing them to fulfil, towards them, all the obligations imposed on them by our treaties, by gratitude, and by provident policy, they have just granted new favors to their commerce, to partake with them the benefits of its navigation, opening to them all the ports in the two worlds; in a word, assimilating them to her own citizens.

Such amicable and disinterested proceedings, should render the federal government, Sir, industrious in seeking at least all the means of serving us as far as circumstances would permit them, but instead of waiting till Congress had taken into consideration the important subjects which should already have occupied them; until they have determined whether the war of liberty, whether the fate of France and her colonies, were indifferent objects for America; until they had decided whether it was the interest of the United States to profit, or not, of the situation in which French magnanimity places them, they have been forward, urged on by I know not what influence, to pursue another conduct. They have multiplied difficulties and embarrassments in my way. Our treaties have been unfavorably interpreted. Arbitrary orders have directed against us the action of the tribunals; indeed, my diplomatic reception excepted, I have met with nothing but disgust and obstacles in the negotiations I have been charged with. . . .

12. Jefferson on Genêt and the British, 1 September 1793.

In spite of a fearful yellow fever epidemic, Jefferson kept at his duties in Philadelphia. Here he kept Madison, who was at his home in Orange County, Virginia, informed of problems with the French, our proper friends, and with the British, who more than ever needed the prod of some commercial restrictions. "Mr. A——" was Fisher Ames, Federalist Representative from Massachusetts. [A. A. Lipscomb and A. E. Bergh, eds., The Writings of Thomas Jefferson (Washington, 1903), IX, 212–13.]

. . . Nothing further has passed with Mr. Genêt, but one of his consuls has committed a pretty serious deed at Boston, by going with an armed force taken from a French frigate in the harbor, and rescuing a vessel out of the hands of the marshal who had arrested her by process from a court of justice; in another instance he kept off the marshal by an armed force from serving a process on a vessel. He is ordered, consequently, to be arrested himself, prosecuted and punished for the rescue, and his exequatur will be revoked. You will see in the newspapers the attack made on our commerce by the British king in his *additional instructions* of June 8. Though we have only newspaper information of it, *provisional* instructions are going to Mr. Pinckney to require a revocation of them, and indemnification for all losses which individuals may sustain by them in the meantime. Of the revocation I have not the least expectation. I shall therefore be for laying the whole business (respecting both nations) before Congress. While I think it impossible they should not approve of what has been done disagreeable to the friendly nation, it will be in their power to soothe them by strong commercial retaliation against the hostile one. Pinching their commerce will be just against themselves, advantageous to us, and conciliatory towards our friends of the hard necessities into which their agent has drawn us. His conduct has given room for the enemies of liberty and of France, to come forward in a state of acrimony against that nation, which they never would have dared to have done. The disapprobation of the agent mingles with the reprehension of his nation, and gives a toleration to that which it never had before. He has still some defenders in Freneau, and Greenlief's paper, and who they are I know not: for even Hutcheson and Dallas give him up. I enclose you a Boston paper, which will give you a specimen of what all the papers are now filled with. You will recognize Mr. A―― under the signature of Camellus. He writes in every week's paper, and generally under different names. This is the first in which he has omitted some furious *incartade* against me. Hutcheson says that Genêt has totally overturned the republican interest in Philadelphia. However, the people going right themselves, if they always see their republican advocates with them, an accidental meeting with the monocrats will not be a coalescence. You will see much said, and again said, about G.'s threat to appeal to the people. I can assure you it is a fact. . . .

13. Madison's Renewed Appeal
for Commercial Restrictions
Against Britain, 14 January 1794.

Citizen Genêt disappeared abruptly from public life; his party fallen and outlawed in France, he married a daughter of Governor Clinton of New York and retired to a farm in that state. Thomas Jefferson retired to Monticello at the end of 1793, leaving behind him a published exposition on United States trade that pointed especially to the British and the unreasonable advantages they enjoyed at our expense. Sup- ported by this report, Madison introduced on 3 January a series of resolutions that would place special duties on im- ports from nations not having commercial treaties with the United States, and the items listed were, of course, those normally imported from Britain. The resolutions also called for raising tonnage duties for nations without treaties (Brit- ain) and lowering them for nations with treaties (France). While debate proceeded on Madison's resolutions, British cruisers, under authorization of new Orders in Council (6 November 1793), were ravaging American commerce in the West Indies. But Madison knew nothing of this when he spoke on 14 January. [*Annals of the Third Congress* (Wash- ington, 1849), pp. 211–213, 215–217. As always with the early Annals, speeches are reported in the past tense and in the third person.]

. . . When the subject was discussed in the first Congress, at New York, it was said that we ought to try the effect of a generous policy towards Great Britain; that we ought to await the close of negotia- tions for explaining and executing the Treaty of Peace. We have now waited a term of more than four years. The Treaty of Peace remains unexecuted on her part, though all pretext for delay has been removed by the steps taken on ours; no treaty of commerce is either in train or in prospect; instead of relaxations in former articles complained of, we suffer new and aggravated violations of our rights. . . .

On the subject of navigation, he observed that we were prohibited by the British laws from carrying to Great Britain the produce of other countries from their ports, or our own produce from the ports of other countries, or the produce of other countries from our own ports, or to send our own produce from our own or other ports in the vessels of other countries. This last restriction was, he observed, felt by the United States at the present moment. It was, indeed, the practice of Great Britain, sometimes to relax her Navigation Act so far, in time of war, as to permit to neutral vessels a circuitous carriage; but, as yet, the act was in full force against the use of them for transporting the produce of the United States.

On the other hand, the laws of the United States allowed Great Britain to bring into their ports any thing she might please, from her own or from other ports, and in her own or in other vessels.

In the trade between the United States and the British West Indies, the vessels of the former were under an absolute prohibition, whilst British vessels in that trade enjoyed all the privileges granted to other, even the most favored nations, in their trade with us. The inequality in this case was the more striking, as it was evident that the West Indies were dependent on the United States for the supplies essential to them, and that the circumstances which secured to the United States this advantage, enabled their vessels to transport the supplies on far better terms than could be done by British vessels.

To illustrate the policy requisite in our commercial intercourse with other nations, he presented a comparative view of the American and foreign tonnage employed in the respective branches of it, from which it appeared that the foreign stood to the American as follows: Spain, 1 to 5; Portugal, 1 to 6; the United Netherlands, 1 to 15; Denmark, 1 to 12; . . . France, 1 to 5; Great Britain, 5 to 1.

It results from these facts, that, in proportion as the trade might be diminished with Great Britain and increased with other nations, would be the probable increase of the American tonnage. It appeared, for example, that, as the trade might pass from British channels into those of France, it would augment our tonnage at the rate of 10 to 1. . . .

Proceeding to the subject of manufactures, he observed that it presented no compensations for the inequalities in the principles and effects of the navigation system.

We consume British manufactures to double the amount of what Britain takes from us, and quadruple the amount of what she actually consumes.

We take everything after it has undergone all the profitable labor that can be bestowed on it. She receives, in return, raw materials, the food of her industry. We send necessaries to her. She sends superfluities to us. We admit everything she pleases to send us, whether of her own or alien production. She refuses not only our manufactures, but the articles we wish most to send her—our wheat and flour, our fish, and our salted provisions. These constitute our best staples for exportation, as her manufactures constitute hers. . . .

It might be regarded (he observed) as a general rule, that, where one nation consumed the necessaries of life produced by another, the consuming nation was dependent on the producing one. The United States were in the fortunate situation of enjoying both these advantages over Great Britain. They supply a part of her dominions with the necessaries of life; they consume superfluities which give bread to her people in another part. Great Britain, therefore, is under a double dependence on the commerce of the United States. She depends on them for what she herself consumes; she depends on them for what they consume. In proportion as a nation manufactures luxuries must be its disadvantage in contests of every sort with its customers. The reason is obvious. What is a luxury to the consumer is a necessary to the manufacturer. By changing a fashion or disappointing a fancy only, bread may be taken from the mouths of thousands whose industry is devoted to the gratification of the artificial wants. He mentioned the case of a petition from a great body of buckle makers, presented a few years ago to the Prince of Wales, complaining of the use of strings instead of buckles in the shoes, and supplicating his Royal Highness, as giving the law to fashions, to save them from want and misery by discontinuing the new one. It was not (he observed) the Prince who petitioned the manufacturers to continue to make the buckles, but the manufacturers who petitioned their customer to buy them. The relation was similar between the American customers and the British manufacturers; and if a law were to pass for putting a stop to the use of their superfluities, or a stop were otherwise to be put to it, it would quickly be seen from which the distress and supplications would flow. Suppose that Great Britain received from us alone the whole of the necessaries she consumes, and that our market alone took off the luxuries with which she paid them: here the dependence would be complete, and we might impose whatever terms we please on the exchange. This, to be sure, is not absolutely the case; but, in proportion as it is the case, her dependence is on us. The West Indies, however, are an example of complete dependence. They cannot subsist without our food. They cannot flourish without our lumber and our use of their rum. On the other hand, we depend on them for not a single necessary, and can supply ourselves with their luxuries from other sources. Sugar is the only article about which there was ever a question; and he was authorized to say that there was not, at the most, one sixth of our consumption supplied from the British islands. In time of war or famine the dependence of the West Indies is felt in all its energy. It is sometimes such as to appeal to our humanity as well as our interest for relief. At this moment the Governor of Jamaica is making proclamation of their distresses. If ever, therefore, there was a case where one country could dictate to another the regulations of trade between them, it is the case of the United States and the British West Indies. And yet the gentleman from South Carolina [Mr. Smith] had considered it as a favor that we were allowed to send our provisions in British bottoms, and in these only, to the West Indies. The favor, reduced to plain language, in the mouth of their planters, would run thus: We will agree to buy your provisions rather than starve, and let you have our rum, which we can sell nowhere else: but we reserve out of this indulgence a monopoly of the carriage to British vessels. . . .

14. Fisher Ames Replies to Madison, 27 January 1794.

The conservative trading interests of New England had no more effective spokesman than Fisher Ames, who wisely limited himself to profit-and-loss arguments and did not, like

Hamilton at this period and himself in a later one, drag in
controversial points about French and British politics. [Seth
Ames, ed., *Works of Fisher Ames* (Boston, 1854), II, 9–16.]

The question lies within this compass, is there any measure proper
to be adopted by Congress, which will have the effect to put our
trade and navigation on a better footing? If there is, it is our undoubted right to adopt it; if by *right* is understood the power of
self-government, which every independent nation possesses, and
our own as completely as any other; it is our duty also, for we are
the depositaries and the guardians of the interests of our constituents, which, on every consideration, ought to be dear to us. I make
no doubt they are so, and that there is a disposition sufficiently
ardent existing in this body to co-operate in any measures for the
advancement of the common good. Indeed, so far as I can judge
from any knowledge I have of human nature, or of the prevailing
spirit of public transactions, that sort of patriotism, which makes us
wish the general prosperity, when our private interest does not
happen to stand in the way, is no uncommon sentiment. In truth,
it is very like self-love, and not much less prevalent. There is little
occasion to excite and inflame it. It is, like self-love, more apt to want
intelligence than zeal. The danger is always, that it will rush blindly
into embarrassments, which a prudent spirit of inquiry might have
prevented, but from which it will scarcely find means to extricate us.
While, therefore, the right, the duty, and the inclination to advance
the trade and navigation of the United States, are acknowledged and
felt by us all, the choice of the proper means to that end is a matter
requiring the most circumspect inquiry, and the most dispassionate
judgment.

After a debate has continued a long time the subject very frequently becomes tiresome before it is exhausted. Arguments, however solid, urged by different speakers, can scarcely fail to render
the discussion both complex and diffusive. Without pretending to
give to my arguments any other merit, I shall aim at simplicity.

We hear it declared that the design of the resolutions is to place
our trade and navigation on a better footing. By better footing, we
are to understand a more profitable one. Profit is a plain word, that
cannot be misunderstood.

We have, to speak in round numbers, twenty million dollars of exports annually. To have the trade of exports on a good footing, means nothing more than to sell them dear; and, consequently, the trade of import on a good footing, is to buy cheap. To put them both on a better footing, is to sell dearer and to buy cheaper than we do at present. If the effect of the resolutions will be to cause our exports to be sold cheaper, and our imports to be bought dearer, our trade will suffer an injury.

It is hard to compute how great the injury would prove; for the first loss of value in the buying dear, and selling cheap, is only the symptom and beginning of the evil, but by no means the measure of it; it will withdraw a great part of the nourishment, that now supplies the wonderful growth of our industry and opulence. The difference may not amount to a great proportion of the price of the articles, but it may reach to the greater part of the profit of the producer; it may have effects in this way which will be of the worst kind, by discouraging the products of our land and industry. It is to this test I propose to bring the resolutions on the table; and if it shall clearly appear, that they tend to cause our exports to be sold cheaper, and our imports to be bought dearer, they cannot escape condemnation. Whatever specious show of advantage may be given them, they deserve to be called aggravations of any real or supposed evils in our commercial system, and not remedies.

I have framed this statement of the question so as to comprehend the whole subject of debate, and at the same time, I confess it was my design to exclude from consideration a number of topics which appear to me totally irrelative to it.

The best answer to many assertions we have heard is, to admit them without proof. We are exhorted to assert our natural rights; to put trade on a respectable footing; to dictate terms of trade to other nations; to engage in a contest of self-denial, and by that, and by shifting our commerce from one country to another, to make our enemies feel the extent of our power. This language, as it respects the proper subject of discussion, means nothing, or what is worse. If our trade is already on a profitable footing, it is on a respectable one. Unless war be our object, it is useless to inquire, what are the dispositions of any government, with whose subjects our merchants deal to the best advantage. While they will smoke our tobacco, and eat our provisions, it is very immaterial, both to the consumer and the producer, what are the politics of the two countries, excepting so far as their quarrels may disturb the benefits of their mutual intercourse.

So far, therefore, as commerce is concerned, the inquiry is, have we a good market?

The good or bad state of our *actual* market is the question. The actual market is everywhere more or less a restricted one, and the natural order of things is displaced by the artificial. Most nations, for reasons of which they alone are the rightful judges, have regulated and restricted their intercourse according to their views of safety and profit. We claim for ourselves the same right, as the acts in our statute book, and the resolutions on the table evince, without holding ourselves accountable to any other nation whatever. The right which we properly claim, and which we properly exercise when we do it prudently and usefully for our nation, is as well established, and has been longer in use in the countries of which we complain, than in our own. If their right is as good as that of Congress, to regulate and restrict, why do we talk of a strenuous exertion of our force, and by dictating terms to nations, who are fancied to be physically dependent on America, to change the policy of nations? It may be very true that their policy is very wise and good for themselves, but not as favorable for us as we could make it, if we could legislate for both sides of the Atlantic.

The extravagant despotism of this language accords very ill with our power to give it effect, or with the affectation of zeal for an unlimited freedom of commerce. Such a state of absolute freedom of commerce never did exist, and it is very much doubted whether it ever will. Were I invested with the trust to legislate for mankind, it is very probable the first act of my authority would be to throw all the restrictive and prohibitory laws of trade into the fire; the resolutions on the table would not be spared. But if I were to do so, it is probable that I should have a quarrel on my hands with every civilized nation. The Dutch would claim the monopoly of the spice trade, for which their ancestors passed their whole lives in warfare. The Spaniards and the Portuguese would be no less obstinate. If we calculate what colony monopolies have cost in wealth, in suffering, and in crimes, we shall say they were dearly purchased.

The English would plead for their navigation act, not as a source of gain, but as an essential means of securing their independence. So many interests would be disturbed, and so many lost, by a violent change from the existing to an unknown order of things; and the mutual relations of nations, in respect to their power and wealth, would suffer such a shock that the idea must be allowed to be perfectly Utopian and wild. But for this country to form the project of changing the policy of nations, and to begin the abolition of restrictions by restrictions of its own, is equally ridiculous and inconsistent.

Let every nation that is really disposed to extend the liberty of commerce, beware of rash and hasty schemes of prohibition. In the affairs of trade, as in most others, we make too many laws. We follow experience too little, and the visions of theorists a great deal too much. Instead of listening to discourses on what the market ought to be, and what the schemes, which always promise much on paper, pretend to make it, let us see what is the actual market for our exports and imports. This will bring vague assertions and sanguine opinions to the test of experience. That rage for theory and system, which would entangle even practical truth in the web of the brain, is the poison of public discussion. One fact is better than two systems.

The terms on which our exports are received in the British market have been accurately examined by a gentleman from South Carolina (Mr. William Smith). Before his statement of facts was made to the committee, it was urged, and with no little warmth, that the system of England indicated her inveteracy towards this country, while that of France, springing from disinterested affection, constituted a claim for gratitude and self-denying measures of retribution.

Since that statement, however, that romantic style, which is so ill adapted to the subject, has been changed. We hear it insinuated that the comparison of the footing of our exports in the markets of France and England, is of no importance; that it is chiefly our object to see how we may assist and extend our commerce. This evasion of the force of the statement, or rather this indirect admission of its authority, establishes it. It will not be pretended that it has been shaken during the debate.

It has been made to appear, beyond contradiction, that the British market for our exports, taken in the aggregate, is a good one; that it is better than the French, and better than any we have, and, for many of our products, the only one.

The whole amount of our exports to the British dominions in the year ending the 30th September, 1790, was nine millions two hundred and forty-six thousand six hundred and six dollars.

But it will be more simple and satisfactory to confine the inquiry to the articles following:

Breadstuff, tobacco, rice, wood, the produce of the fisheries, fish oil, pot and pearl ash, salted meats, indigo, live animals, flaxseed, naval stores, and iron.

The amount of the before-mentioned articles, exported in that same year to the British dominions, was eight millions four hundred and fifty-seven thousand one hundred and seventy-three dollars.

We have heard so much of restriction, of inimical and jealous prohibitions to cramp our trade, it is natural to scrutinize the British system, with the expectation of finding little besides the effects of her selfish and angry policy.

Yet of the great sum of nearly eight millions and a half, the amount of the products before mentioned sold in her markets, two articles only are dutied by way of restriction. Breadstuff is dutied so high in the market of Great Britain, as in times of plenty to exclude it, and this is done from the desire to favor her own farmers. The mover of the resolutions justified the exclusion of our breadstuff from the French West Indies by their permanent regulations, because, he said, they were bound to prefer their own products to those even of the United States. It would seem that the same apology would do for England in her home market. But what will do for the vindication of one nation becomes invective against another. . . .

Thus it appears that nearly seven eights of the exports to the British dominions are received on terms of positive favor. Foreigners, our rivals in the sale of these articles, are either absolutely shut out of their market by prohibitions, or discouraged in their competition with us by higher duties. There is some restriction, it is admitted, but there is, to balance it, a large amount received duty free; and a half goes to the account of privilege and favor. This is better than she treats any other foreign nation. It is better than she treats her own subjects, because they are by this means deprived of a free and open market. It is better than the footing on which France receives either the like articles, or the aggregate of our products. The best proof in the world is, that they are not sent to France. The merchants will find out the best market sooner than we shall. . . .

It may be said, and truly, that Great Britain regards only her own interest in these arrangements; so much the better. If it is her interest to afford to our commerce more encouragement than France gives; if she does this, when she is inveterate against us, as it is alleged, and when we are indulging an avowed hatred towards her, and partiality towards France, it shows that we have very solid ground to rely on. Her interest is, according to this statement, stronger than our passions, stronger than her own, and is the more to be depended on as it cannot be put to any more trying experiment in future. The good will and friendship of nations are hollow foundations to build our systems upon. Mutual interest is a bottom of rock; the fervor of transient sentiments is not better than straw or stubble. Some gentlemen have lamented this distrust of any relation between nations, except an interested one; but the substitution of any other principle could produce little else than the hypocrisy of sentiment, and an instability of affairs. . . .

15. Alexander Hamilton as *Americanus*, 1 February 1794.

In 1793, American partisans of the French Republic had formed political clubs called Democratic Societies in most of the principal towns of the United States. In American politics, they followed the lead of Madison and Jefferson, but often with more zeal and heat than those circumspect and highly-placed statesmen could afford. The Democratic Societies were especially fond of issuing manifestoes in praise of France and in condemnation of her enemies—especially Britain. The Societies survived the fall of Genêt, but their cause was now sufficiently vulnerable for the conservatives to assail it in public. Moved by the threat of Madison's resolutions and by a genuine horror of French politics, Hamilton wrote, under the pseudonym *Americanus,* a series of papers on foreign policy. These efforts show the best and the worst of Hamilton's polemical style—a compound of responsible statesmanship, rhetorical brilliance, and deceptive humbug. The effect of the Federalist critique of Madisonian foreign policy might have been impressive had not word arrived, in February, of Britain's suddenly and secretly imposed warfare on American commerce. [Henry Cabot Lodge, ed., *The Works of Alexander Hamilton* (New York, 1903), V, 74–87.]

An examination into the question how far *regard to the cause of Liberty* ought to induce the United States to take part with France in the present war, is rendered necessary by the efforts which are making to establish an opinion that it ought to have that effect. In order to [form] a right judgment on the point, it is requisite to consider the question under two aspects.

I. Whether the cause of France be truly the cause of Liberty, pursued with justice and humanity, and in a manner likely to crown it with honorable success.

II. Whether the degree of service we could render, by participating in the conflict, was likely to compensate, by its utility to the cause, the evils which would probably flow from it to ourselves.

If either of these questions can be answered in the negative, it will result that the consideration which has been stated ought not to embark us in the war.

A discussion of the first point will not be entered upon. It would involve an examination too complicated for the compass of these papers; and, after all, the subject gives so great scope to opinion, to imagination, to feeling, that little could be expected from argument. The great leading facts are before the public; and by this time most men have drawn their conclusions so firmly, that the issue alone can adjust their differences of opinion. There was a time when all men in this country entertained the same favorable view of the French Revolution. At the present time, they all still unite in the wish that the troubles of France may terminate in the establishment of a free and good government; and dispassionate, well-informed men must equally unite in the doubt whether this be likely to take place under the auspices of those who now govern the affairs of that country. But, agreeing in these two points, there is a great and serious diversity of opinion as to the real merits and probable issue of the French Revolution.

None can deny that the cause of France has been stained by excesses and extravagances, for which it is not easy, if possible, to find a parallel in the history of human affairs, and from which reason and humanity recoil. Yet many find apologies and extenuations with which they satisfy themselves; they still see in the cause of France the cause of liberty; they are still sanguine in the hope that it will be crowned with success; that the French nation will establish for themselves not only a free but a republican government, capable of promoting solidly their happiness. Others, on the contrary, discern no adequate apology for the horrid and disgusting scenes which have been, and continue to be, acted. They conceive that the excesses which have been committed, transcend greatly the measure of those which, with every due allowance for circumstances, were reasonably to have been expected. They perceive in them proofs of atrocious depravity in the most influential leaders of the revolution. They observe that among these, a MARAT [1] and a ROBESPIERRE, assassins still reeking with the blood of their fellow citizens, monsters who outdo the fabled enormities of a *Busiris* and a *Procrustes*, are predominant in influence as well as iniquity. They find everywhere marks of an unexampled dissolution of all the social and moral ties. They see nowhere anything but principles and opinions so wild, so extreme, passions so turbulent, so tempestuous, as almost to forbid the hope of agreement in any rational or well-organized system of government. They conclude that a state of things like this is calculated to extend disgust and disaffection throughout the nation, to nourish more and more a spirit of insurrection and mutiny, facilitating the progress of the invading armies, and exciting in the bowels of France commotions, of which it is impossible to compute the mischief, the duration, or the end; that if by the energy of the national character, and the intrinsic difficulty of the enterprise, the enemies of France shall be compelled to leave her to herself, this

---

[1] This man has lately met a fate which, though the essential interests of society will not permit us to approve, loses its odium in the contemplation of the character.

era may only prove the commencement of greater misfortunes; that after wading through seas of blood, in a furious and sanguinary civil war, France may find herself at length the slave of some victorious Sulla, or Marius, or Caesar: and they draw this afflicting inference from the whole view of the subject, that there is more reason to fear that the CAUSE OF TRUE LIBERTY has received a deep wound in the mismanagements of it, by those who, unfortunately for the French nation, have for a considerable time past maintained an ascendant in its affairs, than to regard the revolution of France in the form it has lately worn, as entitled to the honors due to that sacred and all-important cause, or as a safe bark in which to freight the fortunes, the liberties, and the reputation of this now respectable and happy land.

Without undertaking to determine which of these opposite opinions rests most firmly on the basis of facts, I shall content myself with observing, that if the latter is conceived to have but a tolerable foundation, it is conclusive against the propriety of our engaging in the war, merely through regard for the cause of Liberty. For when we resolve to put so vast a stake upon the chance of the die, we ought at least to be certain that the object for which we hazard is genuine, is substantial, is real.

Let us then proceed to the discussion of the second question. . . .

Though it is not to be doubted, that the people of the United States would hereafter, as heretofore, throw their whole property into a common stock for their common defense against internal invasion or an unprovoked attack, who is there sanguine enough to believe, that large contributions of any kind, could be extracted from them to carry on an external war, voluntarily undertaken for a foreign and speculative purpose?

The expectation were an illusion. Those who may entertain it ought to pause and reflect, whatever enthusiasm might have been infused into a part of the community would quickly yield to more just and sober ideas, inculcated by experience of the burdens and calamities of war. The circuitous logic by which it is attempted to be maintained, that a participation in the war is necessary to the security of our own liberty, would then appear as it truly is, a mere delusion, propagated by bribed incendiaries, or hare-brained en-

thusiasts; and the authors of the delusion would not fail to be execrated as the enemies of the public weal.

The business would move on heavily in its progress, as it was in
its origin impolitic, while the faculty of the government to obtain
pecuniary supplies, would, in the case supposed, be circumscribed
within a narrow compass; levies of men would not be likely to be
more successful. No one would think of detaching the militia for
distant expeditions abroad; and the experiences we have had in our
Indian enterprises do not authorize strong expectations of going
far by voluntary enlistments, where the question is not, as it was
during the last war, the defense of the fundamental rights and essential interests of the whole community. The severe expedient of draft-
ing from the militia, a principal reliance in that war, would put the
authority of the government to a very critical test. . . .

Abandoning, then, as of necessity we must, the idea of aiding
France in Europe, shall we turn our attention to the succor of her
islands? Alas! we should probably have here only to combat their
own internal disorders—to aid Frenchmen against Frenchmen,
whites against blacks, or blacks against whites! If we may judge
from the past conduct of the powers at war with France, their effort
is immediately against herself; her islands are not, in the first instance, a serious object. But grant, as it is not unlikely, that they
become so, is it evident that we can co-operate efficaciously to their
preservation; or if we can, what will this have to do with the preservation of French liberty? The dangers to this arise from the invasion
of foreign armies, carried into the bosom of France—from the still
more formidable assault of civil dissension and the spirit of anarchy.

Shall we attack the islands of the powers opposed to France?

How shall we without a competent fleet carry on the necessary
expeditions for the purpose? Where is such a fleet? How shall we
maintain our conquests after they are made? What influence could
the capture of an island or two have upon the general issue of the
contest? These questions answer themselves—or shall we endeavor
to make a diversion in favor of France, by attacking Canada on the
one side and Florida on the other? This certainly would be the most,
indeed the only eligible mode of aiding France in her war since these
enterprises may be considered as within the compass of our means.

But while this is admitted, it ought not to be regarded as a very easy task. The reduction of the countries in question ought not to be undertaken without considerable forces, for reinforcements could be brought to both those countries from the West India possessions of their respective sovereigns; relying on their naval superiority, they could spare from the islands all the troops which were not necessary for the preservation of their internal tranquility.

These armies are then to be raised and equipped, and to be provided with all the requisite apparatus for operation. Proportionate magazines are to be formed for their accommodation and supply.

Some men, whose fate it is to think loosely, may imagine that a more summary substitute could be found in the militia. But the militia, an excellent auxiliary for internal defense, could not be advantageously employed in distant expeditions, requiring time and perseverance. For these, men regularly engaged for a competent period are indispensable. The conquest of Canada, at least, may with reason be regarded as out of the reach of a militia operation. . . .

But to give the argument its fairest course, I shall take notice of two particulars in respect to which our interference would be more sensibly felt. These are the depredations which our privateers might make upon the commerce of the maritime enemies of France, and what is of far greater consequence, the direct injury which would accrue to that of Great Britain from the interruption of intercourse between the two countries. Considering the shock lately sustained by mercantile credit in that country—the real importance to it of our imports from thence, and our exports thither—the large sums which are due, and in a continual course of remittance from our merchants—a war between the United States and Great Britain could not fail to be seriously distressing to her.

Yet it would be weak to calculate upon a very decisive influence of these circumstances. The public credit of Great Britain has still sufficient energy to enable her to struggle with much partial derangement. Her private credit, manifestly disordered by temporary causes, and propped as it has been by the public purse, seems to have recovered, in a great degree, its impaired tone. Her commerce, too, suddenly interrupted by the breaking out of the war, may be presumed to have resumed its wonted channels, in proportion as the progress of her naval preparations has tended to give it protection. . . .

All who are not willfully blind must see and acknowledge, that this country at present enjoys an unexampled state of prosperity. That war would interrupt it need not be affirmed. We should then by war lose the advantage of that astonishing progress in strength, wealth, and improvement, which we are now making, and which, if continued for a few years, will place our national rights and interests upon immovable foundations. This loss alone would be of infinite moment; it is such a one as no prudent man would encounter but for some clear necessity or some positive duty. If, while Europe is exhausting herself in a destructive war, this country can maintain its peace, the issue will open to us a wide field of advantages, which even imagination can with difficulty compass.

But a check to the progress of our prosperity is not the greatest evil to be anticipated. Considering the naval superiority of the enemies of France, we cannot doubt that our commerce would in a very great degree be annihilated by a war. Our agriculture would of course with our commerce receive a deep wound. The exportations which now continue to animate it could not fail to be essentially diminished. Our mechanics would experience their full share of the common calamity. That lively and profitable industry, which now spreads a smile over all of our cities and towns, would feel an instantaneous and rapid decay.

Nine tenths of our present revenues are derived from commercial duties. Their declension must of course keep pace with that of the trade. A substitute cannot be found in other sources of taxation, without imposing heavy burdens on the people. To support public credit and carry on the war would suppose exactions really grievous. To abandon public credit would be to renounce an important means of carrying on the war; besides the sacrifice of the public creditors and the disgrace of a national bankruptcy.

We will not call in the aid of savage butcheries and depredations to heighten the picture. 'Tis enough to say, that a general Indian war, excited by the united influence of Britain and Spain, would not fail to spread desolation throughout our frontier.

To a people who have so recently and so severely felt the evils of war, little more is necessary than to appeal to their own recollection for their magnitude and extent. . . .

16. George Clinton, Governor of New York, Anticipating War with Canada, 7 April 1794.

Most of the Democratic-Republicans were as determined to remain at peace as Hamilton was, but their leaders emphatically denied the Federalist theory that commercial restrictions would lead to reprisals, deteriorating relations, and finally, like it or not, war. That actually happened between 1807 and 1812, so that much of Hamilton's *Americanus* came to be a sort of fulfilled prophecy. But when Americans heard that perhaps two hundred of their ships with all their cargoes had been seized by British cruisers and condemned as contraband in British West Indian prize courts, there was no longer any question about the intentions of England toward American commerce. She was committing acts of war against us, and the only question before the public was how best to make her stop. Lord Dorchester, British governor of Canada, by no means wanted war, but thought it so certain that he did what his vulnerable position required; he aroused his Indian allies with a warlike speech and demonstrated his intentions further by building a new fort in American territory. He could not defend Canada without Indian allies, and Indians fought best when they believed they could win. Inevitably, citizens of the United States interpreted Dorchester's actions as aggressive and provocative, though in fact they were defensive in intent. The following letter by the Governor of New York demonstrates his quite natural expectation of war. Like the War Hawks of 1812, he also was convinced that Canada was extremely vulnerable and that American troops might easily overrun it. [Clinton to Washington, George Washington Papers, Library of Congress, Vol. 266.]

Dear Sir, I had the honor of receiving your letter of the 31st ultimo a few days ago. Could I have had reason to suppose that the authenticity of Lord Dorchester's Speech to the Indians would have been doubted by any I presume I might have procured at the time the most unquestionable testimony respecting it.

A deputation from the St. Regis Indians arrived at Albany some time in the month of February. Their object was to solicit the state to appoint commissioners to negotiate with their tribes about certain lands they claim within their limits. They informed me that the chiefs of the seven villages of lower Canada were deputed by the western nations (mentioned in his Lordship's speech) to confer with him on the very subject referred to in it, and that some short time before they left home those chiefs had set out for Quebec with this object in view. They also told me a few hours before my getting the copy of the speech that they had received a letter from their chiefs stating that they had conferred with Lord Dorchester and obtained a satisfactory answer, which was afterwards explained to me by them as only meaning an explicit, not a satisfactory answer, but my informants pretended ignorance of its contents. Colonel Louis mentioned to me in confidence his apprehension of a war between the British and Americans and seemed desirous of sending to St. Regis for his wife and children instead of returning there; which he would have done had I not advised him to the contrary and gave him assurances that should a war take place I would take measures for removing his family to Oneida. From these circumstances—from the confidence I reposed in the discernment and integrity of Colonel Udney Hay who transmitted me the speech and from its coincidence with sentiments of Lord Dorchester and Governor Simcoe respecting there being no acknowledged boundary line as avowed to Colonel Samuel Ogden in a report made by him to me, a duplicate whereof I believe was delivered to the Secretary of War. There was no room for doubt left on my mind, and a letter from Colonel Joseph Fay which I now enclose will serve to corroborate the fact.

I shall not fail to pay the earliest attention to the interesting inquiries which you wish me to make and I shall endeavor to conduct them in such a manner as to prevent any alarm and ensure a reliance on the result. In the meantime it may not be amiss to communicate the following circumstances.

Quebec Isle à Noux and St. Johns are the only fortified places in

Lower Canada. Chambly and Montreal are not in a state of defense. All the armed vessels employed on Lake Champlain last war are condemned. A new one has been lately built and now traverses that lake. I have not been able to learn the number of regular troops in that province. The militia is by no means formidable but their numbers I cannot with any accuracy ascertain. The ancient inhabitants are dissatisfied with the government and in case of a rupture I have good reason to believe would be disposed to act in our favor. A proclamation of Lord Dorchester, which I understand has been forwarded to the late Secretary of State evinces in some degree his apprehensions on this subject.

The Vermont militia in the neighborhood of the British lines is formidable. The settlements of Clinton County on our side are recent and dispersed and do not exceed 500 enrolled militia. The greater part of these however are contiguous to the British lines and are well disposed.

As to Upper Canada, the fortresses are much decayed and thinly garrisoned, although they have lately made some repairs to the fort at Niagara. The fort at Oswego is utterly defenseless and only garrisoned by a single incomplete company, and I presume at this moment might be taken without the effusion of a single drop of blood. Governor Simcoe is erecting a fortress at Toronto (now called the City of York) on the west end of Lake Ontario. I understand that he has established in his government a regiment of about 1000 men on [terms] similar to the feudal system and consisting chiefly of the officers and soldiers of the irregular corps that served under the British last war. They occupy the settlement of Catteraqui and consist of about 5000 souls. The regular troops in that province consist of three regiments, one stationed at the City of York, another at Niagara, and the third at Detroit, but neither of them are complete. That at York is greatly reduced by a fever that prevailed among them last summer.

Our nearest settlements to the line of this province are in the vicinity of the Oswego falls, Fort Stanwix, and the Genessee River. The enrolled militia of the counties of Herkimer, Onondaga, and Ontario in which these places are situated consist of between 4 and 5000 men, as nearly as I can compute, but they are very deficient in point of arms, and live considerably dispersed. . . .

17. Monroe Warns Washington to Beware the British Conspiracy, 11 April 1794.

In spite of the provocative actions of British naval commanders, judges of admiralty courts, and Canadian officers, the British government wished to avoid war with the United States in 1794. A new Order in Council of 8 January had made an important distinction between the normal peacetime trade between neutrals and the ports of the French empire and the trade monopolized in times of peace by the French but now thrown open to neutrals in an effort to break British blockades. Thus the British offered to the Americans their famous Rule of 1756, which had declared that a trade prohibited in time of peace would not be considered legitimate in time of war. George Hammond was then authorized to assure the American government that the arbitrary procedures and exasperating delays of the prize courts would be reformed. But Federalist leaders, realizing how badly Anglo-American relations had deteriorated, felt that only a new treaty settling all outstanding disputes could repair the damage. Four Federalist senators urged President Washington to send a special minister to England. Hearing of this, Senator James Monroe of Virginia supposed that the intended minister was Hamilton. His horrified reaction appears fully enough in the following. [George Washington Papers, Library of Congress, Vol. 266.]

. . . That there exists among us a party not to be slighted for its talents or numbers strongly attached to the British monarchy and nation, is a fact which I presume no address has been able to hide from your view. The demonstration of such a party is to be traced from an early period of the government, and is to be found in its uniform partiality for both upon every occasion which occurred; in declarations innumerable both in public and private; but above all in its constant and systematic enmity to the French nation and revolution, of which latter disposition, not to go further back, sufficient proof has been furnished during the present session alone. This single consideration is sufficient to excite a suspicion of the views of this party. To patronize and support Great Britain when offences would not allow it and when her dangerous projects are unmasked and the public mind, wounded with accumulated injuries, is enraged against her, and to discountenance France, the friend and ally of America, in every instance, must have something in view unfriendly to the liberty and safety of these states.

That Colonel Hamilton is a member of this party, active in its councils and devoted to its interests is generally and well known. The particular proofs of it are numerous, positive, and satisfactory. The free disclosure of his sentiments upon these subjects in conversations, anonymous publications (known however to be his) and in his intrigues, have pretty generally explained his true character to the public. 'Tis manifest that at present his prospects are founded upon the British and monarchic interest here alone, and in proportion as the confidence of the country has been withdrawn from him, he has more (entirely, I think) thrown himself upon the support of the former.

Should a person of such character and principles be sent to England, and upon an occasion so attractive of the public notice, it would not only furnish an opportunity for political intrigue against republicanism here and against our connection with France, but, as I have reason to believe, be regarded in America in a light unfavorable to the authority appointing him. Nor could it fail to be viewed by France, in respect to the bias of our public councils, otherwise than with the strongest jealousy and dissatisfaction, and if the mission should not succeed in its object, and a state of things issue so as to require the friendship and co-operation of that country with this, our situation would be as mortifying as it would be alarming. We could neither ask with propriety for aid, nor could she with pleasure grant it afterwards.

That an understanding exists at the present time between this party and the British administration is not improbable, and generally inferred from the late communications of Mr. Pinckney. The footing of intimacy upon which it is known to stand with their minister here, is a circumstance which naturally cherishes the suspicion. . . .

18. George Hammond to Lord Grenville, on a Conversation with Hamilton, 17 April 1794.

Monroe was perfectly correct in saying Hamilton was anti-French and eager for a reconciliation with Britain, but Monroe was altogether wrong in suggesting that Hamilton was pursuing British rather than American interests. The following letter suggests the degree to which Hamilton was an American patriot rather than a British tool. (Henry Adams Transcripts, Library of Congress.)

The executive government would I am persuaded be disposed to persevere in the pacific system which it has hitherto pursued, and which is so essential to its existence, if it was so respected by the people as to be capable of inspiring confidence or of enforcing its own regulations. But it is under the necessity of endeavoring to remedy this defect of confidence by an appearance of submission to the expression of the popular sentiment, and of supplying the want of energy by temporary expedients. But this course of conduct is infinitely too delicate to be always successfully pursued, and if long continued will be ultimately inadequate to either of the objects I have specified. There are indeed at this moment some alarming symptoms that justify but too forcibly this reflection. The democratic societies, to which I have before alluded in one of my letters, and which are precisely analogous in their origin and object to the Jacobin clubs in France, have been for the last three or four months rapidly increasing in the cities, and they are now extending into the country and the different branches are connected with each other through the medium of committees of correspondence. As a specimen of the temper and principles, by which they are governed, I annex to this letter certain resolutions of the Democratic Society established in this city.

In order to allay the popular ferment in some measure, this government within the last three days has dispatched a gentleman of

Philadelphia to the British West Indies for the purpose of instituting in those islands appeals in the cases of such American prizes as may appear to him to have been illegally condemned, and of securing an indemnification on the part of the United States to any individuals who may become sureties for the prosecution of such appeals. In conformity to the same system the President yesterday nominated to the Senate, for the approbation of that body, Mr. Jay as Envoy Extraordinary to Great Britain, and I presume that that nomination will be confirmed either this day or tomorrow. The project of appointing a special commissioner to Great Britain having been (for the causes stated in my dispatch No. 8) for some time in contemplation, I have necessarily been solicitous to obtain some precise knowledge of the objects of the negotiation which will be committed to him. I therefore took occasion from the receipt of your Lordship's last dispatches and in the course of one or two days afterwards to have some conversation with Mr. Hamilton on the subject of them, and I flattered myself that from communicating to him confidentially and informally the very conciliatory explanations, with which your Lordship furnished me, of the instructions of the 6th of November and of the modification of them on the 8th of January, I might derive the right of requiring an equal confidential communication on his part with relation to the special commission in question. I was however much surprised at perceiving that he did not receive those explanations with the cordiality I expected, but entered into a pretty copious recital of the injuries which the commerce of this country had suffered from British cruisers, and into a defense of the consequent claim, which the American citizens had on their government to vindicate their rights. At the same time he added that it was the wish of the government to avoid proceeding to extremities and previously to attempt any mode of amicable negotiation: that for this purpose a person would be sent to the West Indies with a view of instituting appeals in every case of prize which would admit of them, and that, for those cases wherein either from a defect of the law or from any other obstacle of *a like nature,* (such as the necessity of commencing appeals within a *limited* time) that process could not be followed, this government would expect from his Majesty's government an ample compensation for any loss that American citizens might have sustained from the interpretation put on the

instruction of the 6th of November by the judges of the Courts of
Admiralty in the West Indies. And that for the accomplishment of
this last mentioned object, either himself, Mr. King, or Mr. Jay would
be deputed to Great Britain.

This language appearing to me so closely to resemble a doctrine
professed in the House of Representatives, I was determined to obtain a satisfactory explanation of the view of this administration on
the essential point: I therefore desired him to inform me expressly,
whether I was to understand from what he had advanced, that as
an indispensable condition of an amicable arrangement the gentleman who might be employed in this negotiation would be instructed
to require from his Majesty's government a compensation for all
vessels which might have been captured in the British West Indies,
and for the recovery of which appeals could not or might not be
instituted. To this he replied that the gentleman who would be
dispatched to the West Indies, would be directed to abandon all
cases of prize in which the property of the cargo should be satisfactorily proved to be French; but that in the cases in which the
proof should not have been conclusive, or for which appeals could
not be instituted, this government would expect from Great Britain
an indemnification for any loss resulting from the two causes last
assigned, as an indispensable basis of friendly adjustment. In answer
to this explanation, I observed that from my own personal knowledge
I was convinced that artifice to cover property really *French* under
the denomination *American* had been practised to such an extent
and under such disguises that I did not esteem the deficiency of
strictly *legal* proofs in some instances to be presumptive of general
inculpability in others, and that therefore it would require a very
nice criterion to ascertain with accuracy the distinction—that the
instructions of the 6th of November were definite in their import,
were merely declaratory of the system which Great Britain had
pursued in former wars in relation to a traffic carried on by neutral
nations with her enemy in time of war, or which was not tolerated
in peace, and that therefore it was little probable that any prizes
could have been condemned under those instructions which would
not have been condemned under the former system—that no government could presuppose either ignorance or corruption in any
judges employed within its dominions, but that if accusations of this

nature could be *proved* against any of the Judges of the Court of Admiralty in the West Indies, I doubted not that they would be immediately punished—that in *every* possible case his Majesty's government would, I was certain, not throw any impediments in the way of appeals which might be prosecuted—but that in no case could the British government require from the nation a pecuniary compensation to be granted for injuries sustained by the citizens of a neutral power, (if any such had been really sustained) which that government could not contemplate and which it had certainly not authorized—that in every war powers that are neutral must expect to suffer some inconveniences; but that if ever those inconveniences should not be too nicely scrutinized, they certainly should not be so in a war like the present in which (as he had often agreed with me) all the dearest interests of society were involved, and which was a contest between government and disorder, virtue and vice, and religion and impiety, and that in the prosecution of this most just of wars the government and people of Great Britain, united as they were in a common interest beyond the precedent perhaps of any former period (as indeed the war itself was without example) could not be intimidated by any menaces from the exercise of any just principles of carrying it on, which they had found it necessary to establish, and, though they would certainly not violate the rights of neutral powers, they could as certainly not suffer those powers to derive from the distress of our enemy a commerce which, however advantageous it might be to them, would be perhaps more beneficial to our enemy.

Here Mr. Hamilton interrupted me with some degree of heat and remarked that however the government and people of Great Britain might be united against France, he doubted not that when the wrongs which the American commerce had suffered were known in Great Britain, a very powerful party might be raised in that nation in favor of this country. In answer to this insinuation, I contented myself with expressing my astonishment at his indulging a belief, which however it had been entertained by the demagogues of the House of Representatives, and by the uninformed mass of the American Community, I should never have ascribed to him, and thus I dropped the conversation, which thence took another turn, and we parted amicably. . . .

19. Dundas to Dorchester
on Avoiding War,
5 July 1794.

John Jay sailed to England in May, and General Anthony Wayne prepared his army to march into the Northwest Territory and assert United States sovereignty there. Assured that Wayne would not attack the British-held posts near the Canadian border, the British government ordered Lord Dorchester to avoid hostilities. Dorchester was ready to resign; urged to the difficult task of defending Canada, he was now censured for stirring up the Americans by his preparations. Unlike the boisterous Simcoe, however, Dorchester was a peace-loving man, and eventually an appreciative government soothed his feelings. An interesting theme in the following letter is the concern of the home government that the Democratic-Republicans might come to power in the United States. Henry Dundas was Secretary of State for War in the government of William Pitt the Younger. [Henry Adams Transcripts: Canada, 1789–1798. Library of Congress.]

. . . The matters contained in your Lordship's Letter No. 18 and its enclosures are exceedingly important, especially when considered as connected with the present situation, temper, and disposition of the American States. From my several letters to yourself and Major General Clarke, which I take this opportunity of referring to in the margin, as well as from your own sentiments on this subject, your Lordship must be thoroughly impressed with the great consequence which His Majesty's Government attach to the preservation of peace with America, and consequently to the avoiding, if possible, anything like hostilities, in consequence of the disputes concerning the Treaty Line, and the posts on the American side of it, in our possession.

Your Lordship, I observe too, is perfectly well aware, that there exists in the American States a considerable, and certainly a most violent party, whose views seem to be inimical to the real interests of their own government, as well as of ours, and whose objects appear to be, to drive all subsisting matters of dispute between the two countries beyond the bounds of accommodation. Under these circumstances, and without being further informed of the reasons, upon which the measures I am going to mention were founded, I should not deal fairly and candidly by your Lordship, if I were not to express my apprehensions that your answer to the Message from the Indians of the Upper Country, marked G., and your proposing to Colonel Simcoe, in your Lordship's letter to him, marked C., to occupy nearly the same posts on the Miami River, which were demolished after the Peace, may not rather provoke hostilities, than prevent them. On the subject of the above answer to the Indians, I wrote to your Lordship on the 4th ultimo, and with respect to the directions abovementioned for occupying the posts on the Miami River, I am afraid that they extend to what cannot be considered to be within the limits of the post at Detroit, the *immediate* protection of which, as well as of the other posts in our possession, on the American side of the Treaty Line, is the only object to be attended to. . . .

It is to be hoped that the presence of Mr. Jay, who is now here, may lead to a final termination of all disputes, and a perfect good understanding between the two countries. On the other hand it is equally important that, with the most pacific views, on the part of the King's Government every possible provision should be made, which His Majesty's Service will, at this moment, admit of, against the possibility of a contrary disposition on the part of America. I therefore take this opportunity of informing your Lordship, that in addition to the fleet under Admiral Murray, which is on its way to Halifax, as stated in the letter to your Lordship dated the 9th May last, a 44-gun ship and a frigate will sail from hence to Quebec, in the course of this summer, and remain during the winter on that station, for the better protection of the Canadas, and for aiding and assisting your Lordship's operations, if they should ultimately prove necessary.

I have also to inform your Lordship, that 4000 additional stand of arms, with a suitable proportion of ammunition, will be sent as early as possible; and I likewise hope it may be convenient, in the course of the season, to send you some additional landed force, for the further security of the Provinces of Canada.

The broken condition of the Indian Confederacy, as stated in No. 21, and its enclosures, will certainly relieve General Wayne from any material apprehensions on their account. . . .

20. Monroe's Address to the French National Convention, 13 August 1794.

After appointing Jay for the English mission, President Washington had to find a replacement for Gouverneur Morris as Minister to France. He approached men of the pro-French party, in a sort of demonstration that he was still following a policy of neutrality. After James Madison and Robert R. Livingston of New York declined the honor, James Monroe accepted. The European powers would see to it that either he or Jay would fail; both could not succeed. When Federalists heard that Monroe had made a triumphant public speech to the French National Convention they affected to be scandalized; this sort of exhibitionism, they complained, was foreign to correct diplomatic usage and seemed to commit the United States to the principles of the Jacobins. [Stanislaus Murray Hamilton, ed., *The Writings of James Monroe* (New York, 1898–1903), II, 13–15.]

Citizens, President and Representatives of the French People:— My admission into this Assembly, in the presence of the French Nation (for all the citizens of France are represented here) to be recognized as the Representative of the American Republic, impresses me with a degree of sensibility which I cannot express. I consider it as a new proof of that friendship and regard which the French Nation has always shown to their ally, the United States of America.

Republics should approach near to each other. In many respects they all have the same interest. But this is more especially the case with the American and French Republics:—their governments are similar; they both cherish the same principles and rest on the same basis, the equal and inalienable rights of men. The recollection too of common dangers and difficulties will increase their harmony, and cement their union. America had her day of oppression, difficulty and war, but her sons were virtuous and brave and the storm which long clouded her political horizon has passed and left them in the enjoyment of peace, liberty and independence. France our ally and our friend and who aided in the contest, has now embarked in the same noble career; and I am happy to add that whilst the fortitude, magnanimity and heroic valor of her troops, command the admiration and applause of the astonished world, the wisdom and firmness of her councils unite equally in securing the happiest result.

America is not an unfeeling spectator of your affairs in the present crisis. I lay before you in the declarations of every department of our Government, declarations which are founded in the affection of the citizens at large, the most decided proof of her sincere attachment to the liberty, prosperity and happiness of the French Republic. Each branch of Congress, according to the course of proceedings there, has requested the President to make this known to you in its behalf; and in fulfilling the desires of those branches I am instructed to declare to you that he has expressed his own.

In discharging the duties of the office which I am now called on to execute, I promise myself the highest satisfaction; because I well know that whilst I pursue the dictates of my own heart in wishing the liberty and happiness of the French nation, and which I most sincerely do, I speak the sentiments of my own Country; and that by doing everything in my power to preserve and perpetuate the harmony so happily subsisting at present between the two Republics, I shall promote the interest of both. To this great object therefore all my efforts will be directed. If I shall be so fortunate as to succeed in such manner as to merit the approbation of both Republics I shall deem it the happiest event of my life, and return hereafter with a consolation, which those who mean well and have served the cause of liberty alone can feel.

21. The Democratic Society of Lexington, Kentucky, Worries About Diplomacy with Spain, 11 August 1794.

Many a Kentuckian had hoped that George Rogers Clark would liberate Louisiana, but the United States quite properly forbade the raising of a French army from among its own citizens. Dark rumblings continued to come from Kentucky that if the Federal Government could not secure the western people their rights, they might take matters into their own hands. The following document shows the Lexington Democrats in a reflective mood: they are seeking information rather than issuing manifestoes. But the questions they put to John Edwards, one of their United States Senators, are quite revealing—much more so, in fact, than the Senator's answers. These Kentuckians obviously suspect that the insinuations of the foreigners are true—that the United States Government is dominated by eastern interests intent upon retarding the growth of the West. Senator Edwards returned his answers on 3 September. Both questions and answers (largely paraphrased) are in the hand of John Breckinridge, President of the Democratic Society and, among other accomplishments, close friend of Thomas Jefferson. [Breckinridge Family Papers (Library of Congress), XI, 1741–1742.]

What progress was made under the confederated Government in endeavoring to obtain the free use of the Mississippi, and what was the issue of the negotiations on that subject?

A. Know little or nothing of it.

Have you had personal access to the official papers on that subject, during the Confederation, in the hands of the Executive Department?

If so, what appears to have rendered those negotiations ineffectual?

Detail as briefly as possible the rise, progress, and present state of the negotiations with Spain on that subject, since the adoption of the federal constitution.

Have you had personal access to the official papers on that subject, during the present government, in the hands of the Executive department?

A. Certain parts communicated—no copy.

If not, is such personal access to, and inspection thereof, denied to the Senators, or representatives in Congress?

A. No—but must request them.

What were the terms, or propositions held out, or offered to Spain on that subject?

A. Nothing but a discussion of the right.

Was the right asserted?

A. Yes.

Was there any period fixed when Spain should either accede to, or reject the proposition offered by America?

A. Not any that I recollect.

What answer or answers did Spain make to our proposition? On this point be pleased to be as explicit as possible.

A. Can't recollect; that they would go into full and free investigation.

How long was it before she returned an answer at all?

A. Not a single answer until this winter.

Has she given more than one answer; if so, wherein does the second differ from the first, or the third from the second?

A. Can't say—never could be indulged with a copy.

What reasons, objections, or arguments, did Spain urge, for not permitting us to make use of our natural right of navigating the Mississippi?

A. That would be communicating everything, which I cannot.

Were any terms or propositions held out, or offered to Spain derogatory of our right in any degree?

A. No.

Did Spain make any overtures to the Executive or those to whom the negotiations were committed, which if acceded to would have been an infringement, or suspension of our rights? If so, what were those overtures, and when, and to whom made?

A. I am forbid to go into that business.

What answer was given to those overtures by the Executive or its agents?

A. Our ministers required to investigate and settle the right.

We are told by the President's letter to Congress of the 5th of December last, that the negotiations with Spain were *confidential.* What made them so?

A. He (the President) thought them and the Senate thought so too.

In the same letter he promises to communicate *separately* to Congress these *confidential* communications. Did he do so, and what were they?

A. As a member of the Senate, I cannot detail—but if I wished to do so I could not, as they were [illegible].

What prospect is there now, more than there was years ago, of obtaining this right by negotiations?

A. When I went to Philadelphia no account of negotiations at all. It is now going on. Congress have now said we have the right. Also it has been spiritedly stated by the President.

Has Spain showed any disposition to relax, or to acknowledge our right?

A. She seems willing to go into investigation.

What are the objections made at this time by Spain, to an acknowledgment of our right?

Have you any reasons to believe that the President and Senate have fixed upon any period, beyond which negotiations shall not continue?

A. I cannot tell.

In short, from your whole knowledge of this subject are you of opinion that we have a right to ground any *solid* expectations on the present negotiations?

A. I am able to make up an opinion. I don't know the disposition of Spain. I have a hope they will determine finally this season.

Do you believe it to be the earnest wish and desire of the Northern and Eastern politicians in Congress, that we should be invested with this right?

A. Some do, and some I believe do not.

And do you believe they would be perfectly satisfied to see the subject forever languish, under the most hopeless and unavailing negotiations?

A. Not a majority in the Senate.

Have they, or any of them in your hearing, ever expressed a wish, or hope that Western America might continue under its present embarrassments and distress, that its superior natural advantages might not too quickly and strongly allure the inhabitants and weaken the strength of the impoverished and frozen Eastern and Northern states? Do they in short view the rising importance of western America with the eye of patriotic liberality, or with the squint of jealousy and disaffection?

A. To do them justice I can say with candor that a majority of the Senate views the western country with an eye of friendship and expresses their wishes to do everything in their power for its interest and protection. If I at any time should discover a contrary conduct it will be my duty to communicate it to my constituents. . . .

22. Monroe's Alarm at Rumors of Jay's Treaty, 18 December 1794.

The outstanding political problems of several years came to a series of surprising climaxes between the summer of 1794 and the spring of 1796. For the sake of clarity, a brief chronology of these events is desirable. Though Congress had passed a thirty-day embargo in March, 1794, it otherwise set aside Madisonian measures of economic coercion pending the results of Jay's mission, and voted to build a navy. Western discontent climaxed that summer in the famous Whiskey Rebellion in the western districts of Pennsylvania. One source of western discontent, the Indian problem, was spectacularly solved by Anthony Wayne's victory at Fallen Timbers on 20 August. Then, in October, a force of militia called up by the United States marched into western Pennsylvania, and resistance to Federal authority evaporated. Jay completed his negotiations and signed the treaty bearing his name on 19 November, and the Senate finally ratified it, by the minimum two-thirds majority, on 24 June 1795.

The government of Spain, not knowing the precise terms of Jay's Treaty, and fearing that it would lead to a concerted

Anglo-American attack on Florida and Louisiana, now finally
yielded to the demands of the United States both on the
southern boundary question and on the navigation of the
Mississippi. The resulting Treaty of San Lorenzo, 27 October
1795, restored the reputation of the Washington administration in the West. But the peaceful settling of our major disputes with Britain and Spain could leave France only angry
and jealous. Caught in this unpleasant consequence was our
Francophile ambassador, James Monroe. The following letter
reveals how earnestly he tried to prevent the very thing that
happened—the formation of a *de facto* alliance between the
United States and Britain that would place us in a hostile
situation with France. Although Monroe was perfectly correct
about the consequences of Jay's mission, he was perhaps un-
charitable in his estimation of Jay's motives, and of course the
terms of Jay's Treaty were much less astonishing than the
ones rumored in Paris in December, 1794. Monroe's letter
is addressed to Edmund Randolph, who had succeeded Jefferson as Secretary of State. [Hamilton, *Writings of Monroe,*
II, 154–61.]

Dear Sir,

Within a few days past English papers have been received here
stating that Mr. Jay had adjusted the points in controversy between
that country and the United States: in some of those papers it is
stated that Canada is to be ceded with the ports, that privileges
are to be given in the West Indies and other stipulations which imply an alliance offensive and defensive as likewise a commercial
treaty. As this government has always felt uneasiness upon the subject of his mission, and which was greatly mitigated but not entirely
done away by the solemn declarations I had made upon the authority of my instructions, that he had no power other than to demand
the surrender of the ports and compensation for injuries, this recent
intelligence has excited a kind of horror in the minds of those
acquainted with it. And as it will probably get into the papers I
fear the same sensation will be universal for a while. As it is that
this accommodating disposition in the Cabinet of St. James, if it
really exists, is owing to the successes of the French arms, the
good understanding between the United States and this Republic,

and the decisive temper of our government as shown in the move-
ments and letters of Wayne, and which were previously published
in the opposition papers here, it might perhaps be expected from a
just and generous people that we would pursue the adjustment of
our controversy with that country in concert with this: in any event
that we would not bind up ourselves in relation to the present war,
in any manner to prevent us from fulfilling existing stipulations if
called on to execute them, or rendering other service to our ally
which a recollection of past and recent good offices might incline us
to render. But to take advantage of the success of the French arms,
of the good understanding subsisting between this Republic and our
own, and which was created by the dismission of a minister odious
to all France, and the frank declarations which I made in obedience
to my instructions in the presence of the Convention and in the
view of Europe, of our attachment to their welfare and solicitude
for their success, to part the two countries and draw us into the
bosom of our mortal foe, would be an act of perfidy the example of
which was perhaps never seen before.

As yet I have not been spoken to upon this subject by the Committee nor do I expect to be, for *reserve* is the peculiar characteristic of that department, and from which it never deviates except in
cases when the person in whose favor the deviation is, possesses
their entire confidence. Notwithstanding the harmony of opinion
which prevailed among all their parties here, in respect to my political principles and attachment to their nation for services in our
revolution, yet this impenetrable cloak was for some time after my
arrival, assumed even towards myself. It was laid aside by degrees
only and upon their own experience of the verity of these reports:
for so common are the cases of political depravity in the Courts of
the European world, that they act as if nothing else were to be found
any where. If then this report should be entirely discredited, or if
it should be credited, I think I shall not be spoken to. In the former
instance they will not offend me, by letting it be seen that they had
even noticed it. And in the latter as they will be mortified for having
given me a rank in their estimation more elevated than that of other
political agents whom they class generally or in the mass as rascals,
and will consider themselves as duped they will endeavor to hide
it from me. So that in either case 'tis probable I shall not be spoken

to on the subject. If credited it will be seen only by their relapse into the former state of reserve and which the first interview will decide.

On my part I entirely disbelieve it. I can readily conceive that the British administration under the pressure of the French Arms, and the decisive tone of our government will yield the ports and pay us for our losses, or rather it would be the endeavor of that administration to make us pay for it if possible by betraying us into some stipulation which would weaken our connection with France and stain our national character, for they know too well the temper of the public mind to think it possible to connect us with them. And I can also readily conceive that our agent there would be well disposed to harmonize with that administration in an effort to weaken that connection, and in the pursuit of this object he would not be over nice or scrupulous as to the means. But I rest with unshaken confidence in the integrity of the President and in the veracity of the instructions given me to declare that he had no such power. When I contemplate the fixed and steady character of the President, cautious in his measures, but immovable after he has adopted them, jealous of his honor and regardful of his fame, the precious acquirement of great services and of a long and venerable life, I cannot hesitate for a moment in pronouncing that in placing me here he meant what he said, and that I should be the organ of an honest and not a double and perfidious policy. Upon this point I am perfectly at ease. The only point therefore upon which I feel any concern, is the apprehension of the dish which may be prepared for the palate of those who have particular interests with us and which 'tis possible may be contrived with great art by Messrs. Pitt and Jay, the latter of whom would be useful in giving information how such interests might be acted on so as to make it irresistible. And what increases this apprehension is the report that several of the stipulations are provisional, to be executed hereafter whereby the hostage remains in the hands of Great Britain, it being only a project (and of course no violation of instructions in form though absolutely so in fact) to be offered for the approbation of the President and the Senate. By this he would keep his ground in England, harmonize with the administration, and aid it in the means of attacking the integrity of our Councils. Upon this point I have my fears for I knew him play the same game upon the subject of the Mississippi. He was instructed to enter into no *stipulation* which did not open that river and fix the boundaries according to our treaty with Great Britain. He should therefore not have heard a proposition on that subject: on the contrary he absolutely entered into a stipulation which shut the river up, or according to his own language, *forbore the use of it,* and left the boundaries to be settled by Commissaries to be appointed by both countries, as I understand is the case with some of the litigated points in the present case. The analogy in the project reported to be now depending with that I have here recited (and which I have often wished the President would peruse from beginning to the end) together with my own perfect knowledge of the principles and crooked policy of the man disguised under the appearance of great sanctity and decorum, induce me to pay more attention to those papers than I otherwise should do.

If anything of this kind should have taken place I know the dilemma into which you will be all thrown. *The western ports are offered you—compensation for losses—free trade* to the *Islands—* under the protection of the *all-powerful British flag—Canada is* or *will be given* up, whereby the fisheries become more accessible— England will no longer support Spain in favor of the *Mississippi,* etc. This will be resounded in the public papers and the impudence of the British faction become intolerable. But will it not be perceived that whatever is offered cannot be deemed the amicable concession of England but is already your own, attained by the illustrious achievements and prosperous fortunes of your ally, and the decisive of your own councils? Will you take therefore in breach of plighted faith, and expense of our national character, and of an amicable concession of England what may be obtained without loss, and is in truth due to the merits of our ally? I will candidly own that I do not think it in the power of Messrs. Pitt and Jay to succeed in any project they can contrive whereby to weaken our connection with France and put us again under the influence of England, for such would be the case provided that connection was weakened.

I have written freely upon this subject as well to state the report and explain the light in which such an adjustment would be received here, as to put you on your guard in relation to transactions in England, a country which will never smile upon but to deceive you.

'Tis impossible to be closely connected with both these countries if no other considerations prevented from the animosity, and frequent wars that will take place between them, and which must terminate from the superior strength of this in the ruin at least to a certain degree of the other: unless indeed we should now abandon our ally to prop the declining fortunes of hers and our adversary. I write to you in confidence that you will make no improper use of this and that from the necessity of retaining a copy you will excuse its being dressed in the character of a friend.

23. Jay Defends His Treaty, 6 March 1795.

John Jay was just as alarmed at Monroe's behavior in Paris as that stout Republican was at rumors of Jay's diplomatic sellout to the British. The Treaty required approval by the President and ratification by the Senate before it could go into effect. Jay knew it would be vigorously attacked and tried in the following letter to persuade Washington that it was, in the circumstances, a good settlement. [Henry P. Johnston, ed., *The Correspendence and Public Papers of John Jay* (New York, 1893), IV, 162–165.]

Dear Sir: After considering all that I have heard and seen on the subject, it is my opinion that the common and popular (not official) language of America, relative to Great Britain, manifested such a disposition as to create serious apprehensions in this country that we should join with the French in the war; that these apprehensions gave occasion to secret designs, calculated on such an event; that in proportion as your views and counsels became developed, these apprehensions gradually subsided; that my mission was regarded as a strong proof of your desire to preserve peace, and that the perfect and universal confidence reposed in your personal character excluded every doubt of your being sincere; and that this government is not yet entirely convinced that a pacific and conciliatory system will be supported by the inclination and correspondent conduct of the great body of the people. Various circumstances, however, induce me to believe, that the Cabinet ultimately determined to give conciliation a fair experiment, by doing us substantial justice and by consenting to such arrangements favorable to us, as the national interests and habitual prejudices would admit. To relax the navigation act was to alarm those prejudices, and therefore was a measure which required caution and circumspection, especially in the first instance. To break the ice was the difficulty. To enlarge the aperture afterward would be more easy; and it will probably be done, if we should be reasonably temperate and prudent. To admit us into their East and West India dominions, and into all their continental American territories, under any modifications, were decided deviations from their former policy, and tended to shock ancient prejudices. Yet these things have been done. None but a strong administration would have ventured it. These are offerings to conciliation, and include, though not confessedly, satisfaction to our claims of justice.

What passed at Paris on Mr. Monroe's arrival, I am persuaded made a strong and disagreeable impression; and had not your private character prevented those transactions from being imputable in any degree to your orders, I do believe that the system of conciliation would have been instantly abandoned.

What would have succeeded it cannot be easily conjectured; certainly no treaty so favorable to us as the present would then have been attainable. Whatever the American opinion of it may prove to be, the administration here think it very friendly to us; and that it could not in the present moment have been made more so, without exciting great discontent and uneasiness in this country.

The present situation of Great Britain may to us and others appear to be perilous, but the ministry seem to have no such fears. They have been uniformly bent on prosecuting the war with vigor, and since my arrival I have observed no change in that resolution. Even a distinguished leader in the opposition lately told me that the French could not possibly injure the vitals of this country. Let it be infatuation or what it will, the government and the great majority of this nation meant and mean to continue the war. I will mention a striking anecdote.

You have doubtless heard that the merchants concerned in the American trade gave me a dinner. The principal Cabinet Ministers were present, and about two hundred merchants. Many toasts were given. When "The President of the United States" was given, it was proposed to be with three cheers, but they were prolonged (as if by preconcert, but evidently not so) to six. Several other toasts passed with great acclamation, particularly "The wooden walls of Old England." Almost every toast referable to America, and manifesting a desire of conciliation and cordiality, met with general and strong marks of approbation. Towards the conclusion of the feast, I was asked for a toast. I gave a neutral one, viz., "A safe and honorable peace to all the belligerent powers." You cannot conceive how coldly it was received, and though civility induced them to give it three cheers, yet they were so faint and single as most decidely to show that peace was not the thing they wished,—these were *merchants*. Mr. Pinckney was struck as forcibly by it as I was; and we both drew the same conclusions from it. . . .

II

Troubles with France, 1795–1803

1. The Fauchet-Randolph Imbroglio, 31 October 1794 to 19 August 1795.

Joseph Fauchet, successor to Genêt as French Minister to the United States, wrote this routine dispatch to his superiors in the French ministry of foreign affairs on 31 October 1794. His major news concerned the recent suppression of the Whiskey Rebellion, for which he had an understandably partisan interpretation. The letter gained notoriety from two causes: a rather casual aside in it suggested that Edmund Randolph, American Secretary of State and friend of the French Alliance, had asked Fauchet for French money with which to bribe American citizens; and, even worse, the letter fell into the hands of the British on the high seas. They returned it to the United States so that George Hammond could display it to his friend Timothy Pickering, the Anglophile Secretary of War. While the Senate had voted for Jay's Treaty in June, 1795, President Washington had not been able to make up his mind to sign and return the controversial agreement. But when Pickering presented Fauchet's letter in August, it seemed to convince Washington that it was best to risk the destruction of the French Alliance, and come to terms, however unsatisfactory, with Britain. When Washington and his Federalist secretaries called on Randolph to explain Fauchet's letter, Randolph first submitted an angry resignation, and then ran down Fauchet, who was just leaving the country, for an exonerating statement. When Randolph published a lengthy *Vindication*, it merely served to publicize the issue of French efforts to subvert American policy. Fauchet's successor, Pierre Adet, tried the next winter to overturn Jay's Treaty, first by defeating the required money bill in the House and then, when that failed, by advocating the defeat of Federalists in the 1796 elections. This strategy worked to the advantage of the more partisan Federalist leaders, who rather too eagerly denounced the Democratic-Republicans as agents of a foreign power. [Translated from Moncure Daniel Conway, *Omitted Chapters of History Disclosed in the Life and Papers of Edmund Randolph* (New York, 1899), pp. 277–78.]

. . . By means of this new law one can pursue with sudden rigor all of the citizens who have long been refractory; a great number of processes will be sent out, and one waits no doubt for the natural results of such brusque and striking conduct; one prepares already the means of repression in advance of declarations; it was this undoubtedly that Mr. Randolph meant in telling me that under the pretext of giving energy to the government one wanted to introduce absolute power and to detour the President into unpopular paths.

Whether the explosion has been provoked by the government or guided by chance, it is certain that an uprising of a few hundred men, who have not yet been found assembled in arms, and the altogether peaceful meeting of the counties along the fields of Braddock —a meeting which has not been renewed—would not at all be symptoms justifying the raising of so great a force as 15,000 men. Besides, the principles expressed in their public declarations up to now, suggest more that they are high spirits to be soothed than anarchists to be destroyed. But to make public opinion prevail against the demands they have proposed, it was necessary to exaggerate the danger, distort the views of these people, attribute to them the design of uniting with England, alarm the citizens about the fate of the Constitution, while fundamentally the revolution menaces no one but the ministers. One is succeeding by this move; one raises an army. The military and repressive party is Mr. Hamilton's; the peaceful party and the sending of commissioners are due to the influence of Mr. Randolph on the President, whom I believe truly virtuous and the friend of his fellow citizens and of principles.

However, at the same time that one is sure of having an army, it is necessary to assure enough co-operation among the men whose patriotic reputation could influence their party, and whose inertia or tepidity in the present circumstances could compromise the success of plans. Of all the governors who should appear at the head of the requisitions, the one of Pennsylvania enjoys alone the name of Republican: his opinion of the Secretary of the Treasury and his systems has been known as unfavorable. The Secretary of this state has much influence in the popular society of Philadelphia, which in turn influences those of other states: consequently he merits attention. It appears then that these men, with others I have not mentioned, all having without doubt Randolph at their head, are in suspense about deciding on their party. Two or three days before the Proclamation was published, and when, consequently, the cabinet had withheld its measures, Mr. Randolph came to see me with a most harrassed aspect and made to me the overtures about which I told in my [dispatch] no. 6. Thus with some thousands of dollars the Republic could have decided between civil war or peace! Thus the consciences of pretended patriots in America have already a price! It is quite true that the certainty of these conclusions, painful to draw, rest forever in our archives! What will be the old age of this government if it is thus early decrepit? Such, citizen, is the evident consequence of the system of finance conceived by Mr. Hamilton. It has made of the whole people a people pettifogging, speculative, and selfish. Riches alone here command consideration; and because no one wants to be neglected, everyone pursues them.

However, the excess of this sort has not yet passed to the mass of people; the effects of this pernicious system have so far only tainted them lightly. There are still patriots, among whom I am happy to see a worthy ideal of that lofty title. Consult Monroe: he is of this number; he warned me of men whom the currents of events drag like bodies stripped of substance. His friend Madison is also a wise man. Jefferson, on whom the patriots throw their eyes to replace the President, had foreseen the present crisis. He prudently retired, so that he would not be forced in spite of himself to figure in scenes of which sooner or later the secret will be unveiled. . . .

2. Washington's Draft for His Farewell Address, May 1796.

Washington had hoped to retire from public life in 1792 and had asked James Madison to write an appropriate valedictory then. Madison wrote an address praising the Union and warning against selfishness and divisions. But he then joined with other public men to urge Washington to serve a second term. In May, 1796, Washington was certain he would not be a candidate again and he returned to his project of a valedictory. Liking the Madison address as far as it went, Washington added to it his thoughts on the now crucial question of foreign policy and concluded with a rather defensive statement about his own good intentions and pure motives. He sent this material to Hamilton, now as reliable a friend as he had in politics and a man widely regarded as a stylish writer. Hamilton composed the document known as Washington's Farewell Address, retaining the sense of Madison's praise for the Union and of Washington's advice on foreign policy, but happily removing all traces of the self-justification that had appeared in Washington's own draft. Literary fashions change. By those of the present, Washington's style does not seem so bad as he himself regarded it. His ideas on foreign policy are actually clearer in his draft, printed below, than in Hamilton's much more fluent and graceful sentences. Washington's Farewell Address has sometimes served as a sacred text enjoining the United States to isolation. But in 1796, isolation was impossible, for we were still pressed by three European empires in the New World and were dependent upon foreign trade for our prosperity. Washington warned against the subordination of American independence to the designs of a great foreign power; of course, he had France in mind, and his Address was both a defense of his foreign policy and a contribution to the Federalist party in the election of 1796. [John C. Fitzpatrick, ed., *The Writings of George Washington* (Washington, D. C., 1940), XXXV 55–58.]

Had the situation of our public affairs continued to wear the same aspect they assumed at the time the foregoing address was drawn I should not have taken the liberty of troubling you, my fellow citizens, with any new sentiments or with a repetition, more in detail, of those which are therein contained; but considerable changes having taken place both at home and abroad, I shall ask your indulgence while I express with more lively sensibility, the following most ardent wishes of my heart.

That party disputes, among all the friends and lovers of their country may subside, or, as the wisdom of Providence has ordained that men, on the same subjects, shall not always think alike, that charity and benevolence when they happen to differ may so far shed their benign influence as to banish those invectives which proceed from illiberal prejudices and jealousy.

That as the all-wise dispenser of human blessings has favored no nation of the Earth with more abundant, and substantial means of happiness than United America, that we may not be so ungrateful to our Creator; so wanting to ourselves; and so regardless of Posterity, as to dash the cup of beneficence which is thus bountifully offered to our acceptance.

That we may fulfill with the greatest exactitude *all* our engagements, foreign and domestic, to the *utmost* of our abilities whensoever, and in whatsoever manner they are pledged: for in public, as in private life, I am persuaded that honesty will forever be found to be the best policy.

That we may avoid connecting ourselves with the politics of any nation, farther than shall be found necessary to regulate our own trade; in order that commerce may be placed upon a stable footing; our merchants know their rights; and the government the ground on which those rights are to be supported.

That every citizen would take pride in the name of an American, and act as if he felt the importance of the character by considering that we ourselves are now a distinct nation, the dignity of which will be absorbed, if not annihilated, if we enlist ourselves (further than our obligations may require) under the banners of any other nation whatsoever. And moreover, that we would guard against the intrigues of *any* and *every* foreign nation who shall endeavor to intermingle (however covertly and indirectly) in the internal concerns of our country; or who shall attempt to prescribe rules for our policy with any other power, if there be no infraction of our engagements with themselves, as one of the greatest evils that can befall us as a people; for whatever may be their professions, be assured fellow citizens and the event will (as it always has) invariably prove, that nations as well as individuals, act for their own benefit, and not for the benefit of others, unless both interests happen to be assimilated (and when that is the case there requires no contract to bind them together). That all their interferences are calculated to promote the former; and in proportion as they succeed, will render us less independent. In a word, nothing is more certain than that, if we receive favors, we must grant favors; and it is not easy to decide beforehand under such circumstances as we are, on which side the balance will ultimately terminate; but easy indeed is it to foresee that it may involve us in disputes and finally in war, to fulfill political alliances. Whereas, if there be no engagements on our part, we shall be unembarrassed, and at liberty at all times, to act from circumstances, and the dictates of justice, sound policy, and our essential interests.

That we may be always prepared for war, but never unsheath the sword except in self-defense so long as justice and our essential rights, and national respectability can be preserved without it; for without the gift of prophecy, it may safely be pronounced, that if this country can remain in peace 20 years longer, and I devoutly pray that it may do so to the end of time, such in all probability will be its population, riches, and resources, when combined with its peculiarly happy and remote situation from the other quarters of the globe, as to bid defiance, in a just cause, to any earthly power whatsoever.

That whensoever and so long as we profess to be neutral, let our public conduct whatever our private affections may be, accord therewith; without suffering partialities on one hand, or prejudices on the other to control our actions. A contrary practice is not only incompatible with our declarations, but is pregnant with mischief, embarrassing to the Administration, tending to divide us into parties, and ultimately productive of all those evils and horrors which proceed from faction, and above all, that our Union may be as lasting as time; for while we are encircled in one band, we shall possess the strength of a Giant and there will be none who can make us afraid. Divide, and we shall become weak, a prey to foreign intrigues and internal discord, and shall be as miserable and contemptible as we are now enviable and happy. And lastly:

That the several departments of government may be preserved in their utmost constitutional purity, without any attempt of one to encroach on the rights or privileges of another; that the general and state governments may move in their proper orbits; and that the authorities of our own constituting may be respected by ourselves as the most certain means of having them respected by foreigners. . . .

3. The War of Pamphlets: James Thomson Callender Attacks the Federalists, the British, and William Cobbett's *Bloody Buoy*, January, 1797.

James Thomson Callender (1758–1803) was a Scot who fled to the United States when indicted for seditious libel against the British government in 1793. For a while he lived quietly as a reporter of Congressional debates, but by 1796, he was demonstrating his great gifts for polemical writing. No doubt he was inspired to this by the pro-British pamphlets of William Cobbett, whose *Bloody Buoy* represented the French as a brutal nation, and especially so since the outbreak of their revolution. [Callender, *The American Annual Register, or, Historical Memoirs of the United States, for the Year 1796* (Philadelphia, 1797), pp. 213–218.]

During the British war, Mr. Guelph hired every savage tribe of Indians, whom he could get together, to take up the hatchet. They are in use to butcher old and young. They did so all around the inland frontier of the United States. As to the first query, of "any massacres taking place," every campaign produced them. As for women and children being shot, Mrs. Caldwell was so, by a British soldier, and a British officer wanted to burn her body. To say that the blood of *not a single woman* stained the earth is the most notorious of untruths. The Indians were everywhere, within their reach, murdering whole families. . . .

This *Bloody Buoy* deduces the recent degeneracy of the French from their having renounced the Christian religion. The premises and the conclusion are equally unfounded. The character has not degenerated. Religion is not renounced. France has long been full of infidels. Every one acquainted with French writers must know this to be true. Whatever was his subject, almost every author of that country, for the last fifty years, took an early occasion for letting his readers understand that he despised the established religion. This might be very wrong, but such was the fact; and ignorance or falsehood only can deny it. Thus far no degeneracy can be ascribed to Deism, since the latter existed, in all its violence, long before the revolution. It does not appear from the massacres of Carrier, and his accomplices, that the bulk of the people are more barbarous than their neighbors. All the stories in the *Bloody Buoy*, if authentic, are not within one twentieth part so bad as Burke's descriptions of the English in Bengal. The slave-trade evidence given before the House of Commons is equally horrible. The clamor about French barbarities is not excited in this writer by virtuous indignation. It is the yelp of a hireling, who rejoices in the burning of meetinghouses, the ruin of dissenters, and the return of a yellow fever.

America would be in a charming plight, if every man who disbelieved religion were incapable of moral feelings. To the north of Hudson's river, prudence makes infidels in general to be silent. They become more numerous in the middle states. To the south of the Potomac, perhaps one half of the white people have, at bottom, no religion whatever. Yet when the Bostonians had squeezed themselves into a British war, which by prudence might have been for some years averted, the profane province of Virginia rejected a trimming state of friendship and tranquility with Britain. She could easily have preserved her external safety; but she chose to conquer or to perish with her sister Massachusetts. . . . Had Virginia betrayed, on this occasion, a coldness, the revolution must have been stifled. But Virginia took an early and decided part. Her example on either side would have turned the scale; and with a judgment and magnanimity that do her the highest honor, her citizens were next to unanimous. In return, that state is now a favorite object of invective in some newspapers of New England. Menaces of separation are held out. This is the first item in the account current of *gratitude*.

As to the Queen of France, the whole revenues of the United States would not have supported her actual expenses. On printing the Red Book, a disbursement was stated in her name to the amount of six hundred thousand pounds sterling, in favor of one Polignac. The payment was said to be for acting as master of the household to his own wife. This chaste couple were subservient to the personal conveniencies of Antoinette in a capacity too disgraceful for a plainer explanation. Such a character could not be supposed to interest herself in the welfare of any people. To France she was an intolerable scourge. Towards her memory American gratitude needs not to beat high.

As for Louis, if he had been actuated by moral feelings, he would have studied the peace of his own country, instead of plunging her into foreign quarrels. He began a war that loaded his people with dreadful burdens, wasted their commerce, and cost them perhaps a hundred and fifty thousand lives. This was a strange way of showing his benevolence. If he had been the real author of the war with England, these circumstances must have proved him to be a tyrant. Gratitude from this country would have been absurd; since his friendship could only flow from the motive of sacrificing the blood and treasure of his people for the sake of humbling a foreign rival.

But Edmund Burke has, in Dodsley's Annual Register, given the matter a different aspect. He says that the king of France was perhaps the only person in that country averse to the war. Men who looked forward to a revolution were for it. The whole nation considered this as the most precious opening ever to be expected for avenging the black catalogue of insults and injuries from England. The assistance granted to America arose from a complexity of motives. In some, such as Fayette, it was chiefly, perhaps, an instinctive zeal for republican freedom. In others, it was the expectation of a job, or the ambition of charging at the head of a regiment. In *all* there must have glowed an ardent desire to humble the pride of an implacable enemy. The king had not in himself a force of mind capable of rushing into hostility in contradiction to the universal wish of his people. He was a passive agent, borne along on the tide of public enthusiasm. This, though a secret in America, is a fact well known in Europe. Those who pretend the utmost gratitude to him, affect indifference or dislike to the nation at large. The creed of gratitude stands thus.

"I, a New England federalist, or a Hamiltonian, or a friend to order, do slander and hate Virginia, because she was the axletree of the late revolution, and because she might still urge against me a debt of *gratitude*.

"A French army crossed the Atlantic, and saved America from a second seven years of war. They behaved with exemplary discipline, and even decorum. They stole no horses. They burned no barns. They staved no casks of cider. They stripped no infants naked; nor did they hold a bayonet to the breast of its mother. They were not monsters. They were only men. For these troops, I felt no more affection or attachment than for their ramrods. I now hire newspapers to calumniate French armies in the lump. I abhor them, because they have done for themselves what they formerly did for me.

"I am grateful to the late king and queen of France, to whom I never had any disinterested obligations. I profess this gratitude, because my alleged benefactors *cannot now claim a return;* and because this profession gives me an opportunity to blacken the whole French nation, who in reality did so much of my business. This is my *truly federal* system of gratitude.

"I believe that Thomas Paine is the greatest rogue and fool in the universe. My detestation is not founded on his recent ruptures with Christianity, and with General Washington. I had strained every note in the trumpet of reprobation for some years before these circumstances were given to the public. But as they afford a more tenable ground of attack than any one which I could formerly meet with, I now choose to rest my abhorrence chiefly on my horror of blasphemy, and my reverence for Washington.

"I believe this man to be a fool, because he had no business to instruct Americans in the advantages of independence. I think him a traitor, for he had already sworn allegiance to his lawful king. I am offended to hear that an old broken exciseman was able to school the most enlightened nation in the world. I am sorry that Robespierre did not cut off his head. I am glad that he was a twelve-month in jail, and that this confinement has induced an immovable abscess in his side. The French were, at that time, in want of American provisions. They were courting American friendship. Three lines of requisition from the greatest man that ever existed, would have obtained the instant dismissal of Thomas Paine from the Luxembourg.

"Like many better men than myself, I believe that a continental army of twelve hundred soldiers can protect a southwestern frontier of twelve hundred miles. I believe that six American frigates can do, what a British navy of six hundred sail does not choose to attempt. I believe that it is proper to enter into a sixtieth treaty with the Creeks, and to punish an American farmer who pursues them across the boundary line in quest of his horse, his wife, or his children. I believe that he should rather send a dispatch to Philadelphia, and entreat the President to enter into the sixty-first negotiation with these assassins. I believe that when a man has pledged himself to serve his country for nothing, he cannot subsist upon less than twenty-five thousand dollars a year."

4. The War of Pamphlets: William Cobbett as Peter Porcupine, 1797.

Like Callender, Cobbett (1763–1835) had fled to America under British indictment for one of his writings. But though a great critic of governments, Cobbett remained a loyal Englishman, and took the side of Britain against France. This led him to increasingly bolder attacks on the American supporters of France, which he poured out in his newspaper, *Porcupine's Gazette*. One of his targets, Dr. Benjamin Rush, won a libel suit in the Pennsylvania state courts, which virtually forced Cobbett out of business. Returning to England in 1801, he enjoyed a long career as an author and publisher and as an outstanding advocate of popular reforms. Callender, on the other hand, suffered a series of misfortunes that ended with his accidental—or suicidal—death by drowning in Richmond, Virginia. He had been fined and convicted under the Sedition

Act of 1798, and then after Jefferson pardoned him, he felt himself entitled to public office that the President was not willing to grant. Callender then turned to libeling his former patrons and he died a pariah, drunken and destitute. [William Cobbett, A *Bone to Gnaw for the Democrats*. By Peter Porcupine, author of the *Bloody Buoy*, etc. The following excerpts are transcribed from the London edition of 1797, but the work first appeared in Philadelphia.]

Once more the snarling Democratic Crew,
To discontent and mischief ever prone,
Show us their fangs, and gums of crimson hue;
Once more, to stop their mouths, I hurl a BONE.

. . . Let me then ask, What could induce him [i.e., Callender] to come *a' the wa' from Edinborough* to make an attack on poor Old England? And, if this be satisfactorily accounted for, upon principles of domestic philosophy, which teaches us that froth and scum stopped in at one place, will burst out at another, still I must be permitted to ask, What could induce him to imagine, that the citizens of the United States were, in any manner whatever, interested in the affair? What are his adventures in Scotland, and his "narrow escape," to us, who live on this side the Atlantic? What do we care whether his associates, *Ridgway* and *Symmons*, are still in Newgate, or whether they have been translated to Surgeon's Hall? Is it anything to us whether he prefers Charley to George, or George to Charley, any more than whether he used to eat his burgoo with his fingers or with a horn spoon? What are his debts and his misery to us? Just as if we cared whether his posteriors were covered with a pair of breeches, or a kilt, or whether he was literally *sans culotte?* In Great Britain, indeed, his barking might answer some purpose; there he was near the object of his fury; but here he is like a cur howling at the moon.

A newspaper printed at Philadelphia, whose motto is, "The Public Will our Guide;—the Public Good our End," has borne a conspicuous part in "ushering this dark-born devil into light." In one number of that truly puffing print, the speech of a member of Congress is cut asunder in the middle, for the purpose of wedging in an extract from *The Political Progress of Britain* [by J. T. Callender].

The debate was on the propriety of the house's censuring certain societies that had assisted in bringing about an insurrection in the western counties of Pennsylvania, and the extracted morsel, wedged in as above mentioned went to prove that bread was absolutely dearer in Scotland than in England!—Well enough may you stare, reader. Was there ever such an impudent, such a barefaced puff as this since the noble art of puffing has been discovered? . . .

If you want to know the characters of the kings of England, you will find them recorded in history; you will there find the good with the bad; you will find, that they have all had their faults, and most of them their virtues. If you find that some of them were wolves, you will never find that their subjects or their neighbors were lambs. From the same source you will learn, that, ever since the abdication of James II the embers of discontent have been kept alive in Scotland, by the means of ambitious demagogues: you will find that their influence is daily decreasing, but that, like the Anti-federalists in America, they seize every opportunity to exert it, in reviling the government, representing every tax as an an oppression, and exciting the ignorant to insurrection. I wish we could say that a change of air had produced a change of conduct in some of them. The comrades of Muir and Palmer were no sooner landed at New York last year than they began to pick a hole in the coat of the American Government. They openly declared, that it was "tarnished by the last and worst disgrace of a free government," and said that they looked forward to "a more perfect state of Society." . . . I do not say that they had any immediate hand in the western affair: but when rebels from all quarters of the world are received with open arms, as persecuted patriots, it is no wonder that rebellion should be looked upon as patriotism. You will observe (and undoubtedly with a great deal of pleasure) that exertions of such a horrid tendency have not, latterly, had the same effects there, that they have here; but you must nevertheless agree, that it was as prudent and as justifiable in the government of the United States to prosecute the men, who, for a similar crime, are now in the Philadelphia jail, waiting their trials. . . .

Our democrats are continually crying shame on the satellites of Royalty, for carrying on a Crusade against Liberty; when the fact is, the satellites of Liberty are carrying on a Crusade against

Royalty. (Take care, reader, how you confound terms here. Liberty, according to the Democratic Dictionary, does not mean freedom from oppression; it is a very comprehensive term, signifying among other things, slavery, robbery, murder, and blasphemy. Citizen David, painter to the Propagande, has represented Liberty under the form of a Dragon; it is, I suppose for this reason that our democrats cry out against St. George, as "the most dangerous of Liberticides.") If one could recollect all their valorous deeds, on this side the water, since the beginning of 1793, they would make a history far surpassing that of Tom Thumb or Jack the Giant Killer. *The Aurora*, and two or three other prints of that stamp, have served them by way of Backerson: they have been, and are yet, the Saint Bernards and Peter the Hermits of the Crusade.

When they found the Government was not to be bullied into a war, they were upon the point of declaring it themselves against the coalesced Monarchs so well known for their depredations on the purses of all Christendom, and against that old ruffian Harry the Eighth, who is a sort of setter-on of the whole pack. And though this resolve was not put into execution, out of respect for the inviolable and sacred person of his Majesty of clubs, they immediately "let slip the dogs of war," at everything else that bore the name or marks of Royalty.

Their first object of attack was the Stage. Every Royal or Noble character was to be driven into everlasting exile, or, at least, none such was ever to be introduced except by way of degradation. The words your Majesty, My Lord, and the like, were held to be as offensive to the chaste ears of Republicans, as silks, gold lace, painted cheeks and powdered periwigs to their eyes. In short, the highest and lowest titles were to be citizen and citizeness, and the dresses were all to be *à la mode de Paris*. . . .

5. Monroe and the Irish Republicans, February, 1797.

Suggestive light on Monroe's French mission comes from the memoirs of the Irish Republican leader Wolfe Tone, whom Monroe helped in Paris and Philadelphia. Tone's project was to secure the assistance of the French Republic in expelling the British from Ireland; their rule would then be replaced by a democratic United Irish Republic. Monroe gave Tone money, and transmitted his messages. Eventually, the French did attempt to invade and liberate Ireland, but the British easily defeated them. The British also captured Tone and condemned him for treason. Rather than go to the gallows, he cut his own throat. The Irish masses, far from welcoming the French as liberators, regarded them as greater devils than the English. As a representative of the United States government, Monroe had behaved even more rashly than Gouverneur Morris; his political ideals all but smothered prudence. Monroe sheltered Thomas Paine in his home for several months in Paris; it was no doubt there that Tone met the celebrated revolutionary. [*Journals of Theobald Wolfe Tone During His Mission in France* (Dublin, 1846), pp. 95–96.]

Paris, February 22, 1797:

. . . There is now scarcely one of my friends in Ireland but is in prison, and most of them in peril of their lives; for the system of terror is carried as far there as ever it was in France in the time of Robespierre. I think I will call on Carnot today, and propose to him to write Dr. Reynolds, to have some person on whom we can depend, sent over from Ireland, in order to confer with the government here. It may be easily done, and my letter will go in perfect safety by Monroe. Allons!

February 24: This day I called on Monroe, and gave him a letter of eight pages for Dr. Reynolds, in which I give a detailed account of our late expedition, and assure him of the determination of the French government to persevere in our business. I likewise offer him a rapid sketch of the present posture of the great powers of Europe, in order to satisfy him of the permanency of the Republic, together with a brief view of our comparative resources as to England. Finally, I desire him, observing the most profound secrecy and rigid caution, to write to Ireland, and by preference, if possible, to R. S., to send a proper person to Hamburg, addressed to the French resident there, in order to come on to Paris and confer with the Directory. I calculate if nothing extraordinary happens to delay

him, that that person may be here by the middle of July next;
finally, I desire him to assure my friends that we have stronger
hopes than ever of success; and to entreat them, in the meantime, to
remain quiet, and not by a premature explosion, give the English
government a pretext to let loose their dragoons upon them. Such
is the substance of my letter, which I have every reason to hope will
go safe.

March 3: I have [been] introduced to the famous Thomas Paine,
and like him very well. He is vain beyond belief, but he has reason
to be vain, and for my part I forgive him. He has done wonders for
the cause of liberty, both in America and Europe, and I believe him
to be conscientiously an honest man. He converses extremely well;
and I find him wittier in discourse than in his writings, where his
humor is dry enough. He read me some passages from a reply to
the Bishop of Landaff, which he is preparing for the press, in which
he belabors the prelate without mercy. He seems to plume himself more on his theology than his politics, in which I do not agree
with him. I mentioned to him that I had known Burke in England,
and spoke of the shattered state of his mind, in consequence of the
death of his only son Richard. Paine immediately said that it was
The Rights of Man which had broke his heart, and that the death
of his son gave him occasion to develop the chagrin which had
preyed upon him ever since the appearance of that work. . . . But
to return to Paine: he drinks like a fish, a misfortune which I have
known to befall other patriots! I am told that the true time to see
him to advantage is about ten at night, with a bottle of brandy and
water before him, which I can very well conceive. I have not yet had
that advantage, but must contrive if I can, to sup with him at least
one night before I set off for the army.

6. Jefferson's Famous Letter to Mazzei, 24 April 1796 and 14 May 1797.

Thomas Jefferson's retirement at the end of 1793 had been
genuine. He did not try to control the Democratic-Republican
Party from Monticello, but contented himself with occasional
letters and consultations with his friends. He did not, like

Hamilton, enlarge the circle of his enemies by engaging in newspaper polemics. But quite unintentionally, he placed some of his controversial opinions before the world by submitting them to the Italian Republican, Philip Mazzei. Mazzei published Jefferson's letters as translated into Italian, the French picked it up and published it in further translation, and the Federalists then published it in New York City, 14 May 1797, as translated from French. By this time, Jefferson had been drawn from his retirement into the vice-presidency. The appearance of the letter embarrassed him, the more so because the French added a sentence not contained in the original: "It suffices that we arrest the progress of that system of ingratitude and injustice towards France, from which they would alienate us, to bring us under British influence . . ." [Paul L. Ford, ed., *The Writings of Thomas Jefferson* (New York, 1896) VII, 72–77.]

The aspect of our politics has wonderfully changed since you left us. In place of that noble love of liberty and republican government which carried us triumphantly through the war, an Anglican, monarchical, and aristocratical party has sprung up, whose avowed object is to draw over us the substance, as they have already done the forms, of the British government. The main body of our citizens, however, remain true to their republican principles; the whole landed interest is republican, and so is a great mass of talents. Against us are the Executive, the Judiciary, two out of three branches of the Legislature, all the officers of the government, all who want to be officers, all timid men who prefer the calm of despotism to the boisterous sea of liberty, British merchants and Americans trading on British capitals, speculators and holders in the banks and public funds, a contrivance invented for the purposes of corruption, and for assimilating us in all things to the rotten as well as the sound parts of the British model. It would give you a fever were I to name to you the apostates who have gone over to these heresies, men who were Samsons in the field and Solomons in the council, but who have had their heads shorn by the harlot England. In short, we are likely to preserve the liberty we have obtained only by unremitting labors and perils. But we shall preserve them; and our mass of weight and wealth on the good side is so great, as to leave no danger that force will ever be attempted against us. We have only to awake and snap the Lilliputian cords with which they have been entangling us during the first sleep which succeeded our labors. . . .

7. John Adams's Special Message to Congress, 16 May 1797.

Since 1793, the French had been seizing American ships, arguing justly that if the United States acquiesced in British interference with its neutral trade, it must not expect the French to allow us freely to trade with their enemies. American Democratic-Republicans argued that the British faction in the United States had forced the French into a hostile position. The Federalists could reply that the French would not allow us to be neutral and independent, and when the moderate Charles Cotesworth Pinckney arrived in Paris to replace Monroe, the French Directory ordered him out of the country. With diplomatic relations broken and French attacks on American shipping increasing in Europe and in the Caribbean, John Adams felt obliged to call an emergency session of Congress. Vain and sensitive to criticism to begin with, Adams was in the difficult position of coping with an undeclared war for which much of the country blamed his government rather than the foreign aggressors. [James D. Richardson, ed., *A Compilation of the Messages and Papers of the Presidents,* (Washington, D. C., 1909), I, 233–38.]

Gentlemen of the Senate and Gentlemen of the House of Representatives:

The personal inconveniences to the members of the Senate and of the House of Representatives in leaving their families and private affairs at this season of the year are so obvious that I the more regret the extraordinary occasion which has rendered the convention of Congress indispensable.

It would have afforded me the highest satisfaction to have been able to congratulate you on a restoration of peace to the nations of

Europe whose animosities have endangered our tranquility; but we have still abundant cause of gratitude to the Supreme Dispenser of National Blessings for general health and promising seasons, for domestic and social happiness, for the rapid progress and ample acquisitions of industry through extensive territories, for civil, political, and religious liberty. While other states are desolated with foreign war or convulsed with intestine divisions, the United States present the pleasing prospect of a nation governed by mild and equal laws, generally satisfied with the possession of their rights, neither envying the advantages nor fearing the power of other nations, solicitous only for the maintenance of order and justice and the preservation of liberty, increasing daily in their attachment to a system of government in proportion to their experience of its utility, yielding a ready and general obedience to laws flowing from the reason and resting on the only solid foundation—the affections of the people.

It is with extreme regret that I shall be obliged to turn your thoughts to other circumstances, which admonish us that some of these felicities may not be lasting. But if the tide of our prosperity is full and a reflux commencing, a vigilant circumspection becomes us, that we may meet our reverses with fortitude and extricate ourselves from their consequences with all the skill we possess and all the efforts in our power.

In giving to Congress information of the state of the Union and recommending to their consideration such measures as appear to me to be necessary or expedient, according to my constitutional duty, the causes and the objects of the present extraordinary session will be explained.

After the President of the United States received information that the French Government had expressed serious discontents at some proceedings of the Government of these States said to affect the interests of France, he thought it expedient to send to that country a new minister, fully instructed to enter on such amicable discussions and to give such candid explanations as might happily remove the discontents and suspicions of the French Government and vindicate the conduct of the United States. For this purpose he selected from among his fellow citizens a character whose integrity, talents, experience, and services had placed him in the rank of the most esteemed and respected in the nation. The direct object of his mission was expressed in his letter of credence to the French Republic, being "to maintain that good understanding which from the commencement of the alliance had subsisted between the two nations, and to efface unfavorable impressions, banish suspicions, and restore that cordiality which was at once the evidence and pledge of a friendly union." And his instructions were to the same effect, "faithfully to represent the disposition of the Government and people of the United States (their disposition being one), to remove jealousies and obviate complaints by showing that they were groundless, to restore that mutual confidence which had been so unfortunately and injuriously impaired, and to explain the relative interests of both countries and the real sentiments of his own."

A minister thus specially commissioned, it was expected, would have proved the instrument of restoring mutual confidence between the two Republics. The first step of the French Government corresponded with that expectation. A few days before his arrival at Paris the French minister of foreign relations informed the American minister then resident at Paris of the formalities to be observed by himself in taking leave, and by his successor preparatory to his reception. These formalities they observed, and on the 9th of December presented officially to the minister of foreign relations, the one a copy of his letters of recall, the other a copy of his letters of credence.

These were laid before the Executive Directory. Two days afterwards the minister of foreign relations informed the recalled American minister that the Executive Directory had determined not to receive another minister plenipotentiary from the United States until after the redress of grievances demanded of the American Government, and which the French Republic had a right to expect from it. The American minister immediately endeavored to ascertain whether by refusing to receive him it was intended that he should retire from the territories of the French Republic, and verbal answers were given that such was the intention of the Directory. For his own justification he desired a written answer, but obtained none until toward the last of January, when, receiving notice in writing to quit the territories of the Republic, he proceeded to Amsterdam, where he proposed to wait for instruction from this Government. During his residence at Paris cards of hospitality were refused him, and he was threatened with being subjected to the jurisdiction of the minister of police; but with becoming firmness he insisted on the protection of the law of nations due to him as the known minister of a foreign power. You will derive further information from his dispatches, which will be laid before you.

As it is often necessary that nations should treat for the mutual advantage of their affairs, and especially to accommodate and terminate differences, and as they can treat only by ministers, the right of embassy is well known and established by the law and usage of nations. The refusal on the part of France to receive our minister is, then, the denial of a right; but the refusal to receive him until we have acceded to their demands without discussion and without investigation is to treat us neither as allies nor as friends, nor as a sovereign state.

With this conduct of the French Government it will be proper to take into view the public audience given to the late minister of the United States on his taking leave of the Executive Directory. The speech of the President discloses sentiments more alarming than the refusal of a minister, because more dangerous to our independence and union, and at the same time studiously marked with indignities toward the Government of the United States. It evinces a disposition to separate the people of the United States from the Government, to persuade them that they have different affections, principles, and interests from those of their fellow citizens whom they themselves have chosen to manage their common concerns, and thus to produce divisions fatal to our peace. Such attempts ought to be repelled with a decision which shall convince France and the world that we are not a degraded people, humiliated under a colonial spirit of fear and sense of inferiority, fitted to be the miserable instruments of foreign influence, and regardless of national honor, character, and interest.

I should have been happy to have thrown a veil over these transactions if it had been possible to conceal them; but they have passed on the great theater of the world, in the face of all Europe and

America, and with such circumstances of publicity and solemnity
that they can not be disguised and will not soon be forgotten. They
have inflicted a wound in the American breast. It is my sincere desire, however, that it may be healed.

It is my sincere desire, and in this I presume I concur with you
and with our constituents, to preserve peace and friendship with all
nations; and believing that neither the honor nor the interest of the
United States absolutely forbid the repetition of advances for securing these desirable objects with France, I shall institute a fresh
attempt at negotiation, and shall not fail to promote and accelerate
an accommodation on terms compatible with the rights, duties, interests, and honor of the nation. If we have committed errors, and
these can be demonstrated, we shall be willing to correct them; if
we have done injuries, we shall be willing on conviction to redress
them; and equal measures of justice we have a right to expect from
France and every other nation.

The diplomatic intercourse between the United States and France
being at present suspended, the Government has no means of obtaining official information from that country. Nevertheless, there
is reason to believe that the Executive Directory passed a decree on
the 2d of March last contravening in part the treaty of amity and
commerce of 1778, injurious to our lawful commerce and endangering the lives of our citizens. A copy of this decree will be laid before
you.

While we are endeavoring to adjust all our differences with
France by amicable negotiation, the progress of the war in Europe,
the depredations on our commerce, the personal injuries to our
citizens, and the general complexion of affairs render it my indispensable duty to recommend to your consideration effectual measures of defense.

The commerce of the United States has become an interesting object of attention, whether we consider it in relation to the wealth
and finances or the strength and resources of the nation. With a
seacoast of near 2,000 miles in extent, opening a wide field for fisheries, navigation, and commerce, a great portion of our citizens
naturally apply their industry and enterprise to these objects. Any
serious and permanent injury to commerce would not fail to pro-

duce the most embarrassing disorders. To prevent it from being undermined and destroyed it is essential that it receive an adequate protection.

The naval establishment must occur to every man who considers the injuries committed on our commerce, the insults offered to our citizens, and the description of vessels by which these abuses have been practiced. As the sufferings of our mercantile and seafaring citizens can not be ascribed to the omission of duties demandable, considering the neutral situation of our country, they are to be attributed to the hope of impunity arising from a supposed inability on our part to afford protection. To resist the consequences of such impressions on the minds of foreign nations and to guard against the degradation and servility which they must finally stamp on the American character is an important duty of Government.

A naval power, next to the militia, is the natural defense of the United States. The experience of the last war would be sufficient to show that a moderate naval force, such as would be easily within the present abilities of the Union, would have been sufficient to have baffled many formidable transportations of troops from one State to another, which were then practiced. Our seacoasts, from their great extent, are more easily annoyed and more easily defended by a naval force than any other. With all the materials our country abounds; in skill our naval architects and navigators are equal to any, and commanders and seamen will not be wanting.

But although the establishment of a permanent system of naval defense appears to be requisite, I am sensible it cannot be formed so speedily and extensively as the present crisis demands. Hitherto I have thought proper to prevent the sailing of armed vessels except on voyages to the East Indies, where general usage and the danger from pirates appeared to render the permission proper. Yet the restriction has originated solely from a wish to prevent collisions with the powers at war, contravening the act of Congress of June, 1794, and not from any doubt entertained by me of the policy and propriety of permitting our vessels to employ means of defense while engaged in a lawful foreign commerce. It remains for Congress to prescribe such rules and regulations as will enable our seafaring citizens to defend themselves against violations of the law of nations, and at the same time restrain them from committing acts of hostility against the powers at war. In addition to this voluntary provision for defense by individual citizens, it appears to me necessary to equip the frigates, and provide other vessels of inferior force, to take under convoy such merchant vessels as shall remain unarmed.

The greater part of the cruisers whose depredations have been most injurious have been built and some of them partially equipped in the United States. Although an effectual remedy may be attended with difficulty, yet I have thought it my duty to present the subject generally to your consideration. If a mode can be devised by the wisdom of Congress to prevent the resources of the United States from being converted into the means of annoying our trade, a great evil will be prevented. With the same view, I think it proper to mention that some of our citizens resident abroad have fitted out privateers, and others have voluntarily taken the command, or entered on board of them, and committed spoliations on the commerce of the United States. Such unnatural and iniquitous practices can be restrained only by severe punishments.

But besides a protection of our commerce on the seas, I think it highly necessary to protect it at home, where it is collected in our most important ports. The distance of the United States from Europe and the well-known promptitude, ardor, and courage of the people in defense of their country happily diminish the probability of invasion. Nevertheless, to guard against sudden and predatory incursions the situation of some of our principal seaports demands your consideration. And as our country is vulnerable in other interests besides those of its commerce, you will seriously deliberate whether the means of general defense ought not to be increased by an addition to the regular artillery and cavalry, and by arrangements for forming a provisional army.

With the same view, and as a measure which, even in a time of universal peace, ought not to be neglected, I recommend to your consideration a revision of the laws for organizing, arming, and disciplining the militia, to render that natural and safe defense of the country efficacious.

Although it is very true that we ought not to involve ourselves in the political system of Europe, but to keep ourselves always distinct and separate from it if we can, yet to effect this separation, early, punctual, and continual information of the current chain of

events and of the political projects in contemplation is no less
necessary than if we were directly concerned in them. It is necessary,
in order to the discovery of the efforts made to draw us into the
vortex, in season to make preparations against them. However we
may consider ourselves, the maritime and commercial powers of
the world will consider the United States of America as forming a
weight in that balance of power in Europe which never can be
forgotten or neglected. It would not only be against our interest, but
it would be doing wrong to one half of Europe, at least, if we should
voluntarily throw ourselves into either scale. It is a natural policy
for a nation that studies to be neutral to consult with other nations
engaged in the same studies and pursuits. At the same time that
measures might be pursued with this view, our treaties with Prussia
and Sweden, one of which is expired and the other near expiring,
might be renewed. . . .

8. Federalists and Revolutionary Plots: Miranda to Hamilton, 6 April 1798.

The rest of 1797 and 1798 saw American-French relations
deteriorate further. Armed merchantmen and warships from
the United States battled French cruisers in the Caribbean
while increasingly partisan Federalists passed the repressive
Alien and Sedition Acts. Alexander Hamilton was busy organizing the Federal army and hoping for a grand military and
commercial alliance with the British. Their strength combined, the United States and Britain would sweep France and
Spain from all the Americas and divide the riches of the
hemisphere between themselves. Hamilton briefly considered
co-operating with the perennial liberator of Latin America,
Francisco de Miranda, but decided such co-operation would
be useless. Nevertheless, Miranda continued to have a following among the Federalists, several of whom actually gave him,
in 1806, money and equipment to launch an insurrection. Such
behavior by the Federalists proved that their criticism of the
revolutionary process as dangerous and destructive came not
from a conservative humanitarianism, but from the instinct
for survival. They felt threatened by the French Revolution.

But with Spain a satellite of France, revolutions in her colonies would, at the very least, distract the enemies of England and, at best, open the rich markets of Latin America to British and American trade. Miranda wrote Hamilton from London, where he was seeking British assistance. Rufus King, our minister to England, helped Miranda in much the way that Monroe had helped Wolfe Tone. Hamilton was entirely sympathetic to the liberation of Latin America, but did not believe that Miranda was the man for the job. [Translated from the original in the Alexander Hamilton Papers (Library of Congress), XXX, 4219.]

This will be delivered to you, my dear and honored friend, by my compatriot, Don Pedro Josef de Caro, bearer of dispatches of the highest importance for the President of the United States; he will tell you confidentially what you wish to learn of this subject. It would appear that the moment of our emancipation approaches, and that the establishment of liberty on all the continent of the New World is entrusted to us by Providence. The only danger that I foresee is the introduction of French principles, which would poison liberty in its cradle, and conclude by soon destroying yours. But if we take wise precautions in time all should succeed very well. He will show you my instructions in this respect, and you may add that which I might have overlooked.

We are agreed in advance on a mixed form of government, which would seem to me most agreeable to the country. I shall have the honor of submitting it to you soon; but I warn you that we shall wish to have you with us for this important object, and that this is the wish of those of my countrymen to whom I have spoken about this affair. My friend, I hope that you will not refuse when the moment arrives . . . your Greek predecessor Solon would not have done less, I am sure, and it may be possible that I shall soon take you myself [to South America].

There is among you another person whose reputation is known to me who could, I believe, very well render us very important services in the military party; this is General *H. Lee* of Virginia. As I received at the beginning of the Revolution in France (by my friend Colonel N. Smith) a letter from him proposing to be of service to the republic then, I flatter myself that he would not refuse us now, when it is a question of true liberty, which we all love, and of the happiness of his compatriots of Peru and Mexico. Will you do me the favor of presenting this to him in advance, so that he can prepare himself to accompany us, recommending to him always all the reserve that is indispensable. Would our friend Knox wish to come? I would be delighted, but I fear not.

In conclusion, bear yourself well my dear friend—send me your news, addressed in care of Mr. King, your minister plenipotentiary here. Present my respectful compliments to Mrs. Hamilton, and believe me always with an inviolable attachment your sincere friend.

F. de Miranda

9. Timothy Pickering on the Deceitful Republicans, 9 April 1798.

Alexander Hamilton retired from the Treasury at the end of 1795, but continued to influence policy through close association and sympathy with his successor, Oliver Wolcott, and Timothy Pickering, Randolph's successor as Secretary of State. When Hamilton became *de facto* head of the army, the nation suffered a grave imbalance in its leadership, for these men represented the views of a minority. It is perfectly true that Pickering, Wolcott, and Hamilton were no more warped in their politics than Monroe, John Taylor of Carolina, or Matthew Lyon of Vermont. But the doctrinaire or fanatic Democratic-Republicans never served as chief secretaries of the national government or as military leaders. Monroe ultimately did, but by that time, he had become one of the most responsible of American leaders. Pickering wrote the following letter in Philadelphia, still the Federal capital, to Hamilton, in New York City, just after the publication of the notorious XYZ papers, which documented the latest French insults to the peaceful efforts of American diplomacy. [Hamilton Papers, XXX, 4224.]

Dear Sir, This morning the dispatches of our envoys are published, and I enclose a copy. . . .

You will readily imagine what apologies our internal enemies make for the French Government. Jefferson says that the Directory are not implicated in the villainy and corruption displayed in these dispatches—or at least that these offer no proof against them. Bache's paper of last Saturday says "That M. Talleyrand is notoriously anti-republican, that he was the intimate friend of Mr. Hamilton, Mr. King and other great federalists, and that it is probably owing to the determined hostility which he discovered in them toward France, that the Government of that country consider us only as objects of plunder." . . .

10. Further Reports on the "Internal Enemy," 11 April 1798.

> The following letter was written by David Ford, a minor Federalist of New Jersey, to Alexander Hamilton. It concluded with the advice that those everlasting Hamiltonian favorites, the "men of wealth and talents," should invest some of their ample wealth in counterpropaganda in the rural districts of America, where, after all, most of the voters lived. [Hamilton Papers, XXX, 4225–26.]

Dear Sir, The endeavors and industry of the enemies of America, the French faction, is becoming every day greater—nothing bounds their ambition, but a total overthrow of the Government. To this end every possible scheme of villainy is used—now under the specious pretence of Peace, they are in every part of this state, endeavoring to raise distrust towards the government. Our town meetings in this part of New Jersey are held by law the 2d Monday in April. On that day by a concerted plan the demons came forward at almost every poll and surprised the people with a remonstrance as they called it against war. These in general were drawn so as to criminate our own Chief Magistrate and those who support him, and in most places the idea of its being a petition for peace, obtained it support. All this is a prelude to the succeeding election in October, for members of Congress.

But the greatest evil that pervades our country is the country presses. There have been many of them set up and supported by the Democratic Party in different places, and those not actually raised by their private collections of money have been as it were seized, or hired, by the party to retail scandal against the Government, so that nine tenths of the presses out of the great towns in America to the south of the Hudson are Democratic and most of them in direct pay—or by influences. While the opposers of the government are doing all this and ten times as much by misrepresentation, the wealth, information, and abilities of our country are not excited at all, or very little indeed. But not at all to my knowledge by establishing and supporting with money good presses throughout the country whereby the people would be truly informed, for I am bold to say if they knew the truth the French faction must sink. . . .

11. The Reverend Timothy Dwight Exposes the History of Infidelity, 4 July 1798.

To the devout Christians of New England, the wars of the French Revolution contained more than the traditional imperial struggles for territory and markets; they also embodied the efforts of the Powers of Darkness to overthrow God's True Church. The decade of the 1790's saw, along with the rise of revolutionary France, the elevation of Timothy Dwight (1752–1817) to the presidency of Yale College and to a position of unchallenged eminence among conservative New England preachers. In education a man of wide sympathies and an influential reformer, Dwight was an authentic conservative in theology and politics, as befitted a grandson of Jonathan Edwards. The Independence Day sermon from which the following selection is taken starts off with a long and ingenious explication of modern history as fulfillment of the prophecies in the Book of Revelation. [*The Duty of Americans, at the Present Crisis* . . . (New Haven, 1798), pp. 8–13.]

About the year 1728, Voltaire, so celebrated for his wit and brilliancy, and not less distinguished for his hatred of Christianity and his abandonment of principle, formed a systematical design to destroy Christianity, and to introduce in its stead a general diffusion of irreligion and atheism. For this purpose he associated with himself Frederic the II, King of Prussia, and Messrs. D'Alembert and Diderot, the principal compilers of the Encyclopédie; all men of talents, atheists, and in the like manner abandoned. The principal parts of this system were, 1st. The compilation of the Encyclopédie (the celebrated French Dictionary of Arts and Sciences, in which articles of Theology were speciously and decently written, but, by references artfully made to other articles, all the truth of the former was entirely and insidiously overthrown to most readers, by the sophistry of the latter); in which with great art and insidiousness the doctrines of Natural as well as Christian Theology were rendered absurd and ridiculous; and the mind of the reader was insensibly steeled against conviction and duty. 2. The overthrow of the religious orders in Catholic countries; a step essentially necessary to the destruction of the religion professed in those countries. 3. The establishment of a sect of philosophists to serve, it is presumed, as a conclave, a rallying point, for all their followers. 4. The appropriation to themselves, and their disciples, of the places and honors of members of the French Academy, the most respectable literary society in France, and always considered as containing none but men of prime learning and talents. In this way they designed to hold out themselves, and their friends, as the only persons of great literary and intellectual distinction in that country, and to dictate all literary opinions to the nation. 5. The fabrication of books of all kinds against Christianity, especially such as excite doubt, and generate contempt and derision.

Of these they issued, by themselves and their friends, who early became numerous, an immense number; so printed, as to be purchased for little or nothing, and so written, as to catch the feelings, and steal upon the approbation, of every class of men. 6. The formation of a secret Academy, of which Voltaire was the standing president, and in which books were formed, altered, forged, imputed as posthumous to deceased writers of reputation, and sent abroad with the weight of their names. These were printed and circulated, at the lowest price, through all classes of men, in an uninterrupted succession, and through every part of the kingdom.

Nor were the labors of this Academy confined to religion. They attacked also morality and government, unhinged gradually the minds of men, and destroyed their reverence for everything heretofore esteemed sacred.

In the meantime, the Masonic Societies, which had been originally instituted for convivial and friendly purposes only, were, especially in France and Germany, made the professed scenes of debate concerning religion, morality, and government, by these philosophists, who had in great numbers become Masons. For such debate the legalized existence of Masonry, its profound secrecy, its solemn and mystic rites and symbols, its mutual correspondence, and its extension through most civilized countries, furnished the greatest advantages. All here was free, safe, and calculated to encourage the boldest excursions of restless opinion and impatient ardor, and to make and fix the deepest impressions. Here, and in no other place, under such arbitrary governments, could every innovator in these important subjects utter every sentiment, however daring, and attack every doctrine and institution, however guarded by law or sanctity. In the secure and unrestrained debates of the lodge, every novel, licentious, and alarming opinion was resolutely advanced. Minds, already tinged with philosophism, were here speedily blackened with a deep and deadly dye; and those, which came fresh and innocent to the scene of contamination, became early and irremediably corrupted. A stubborn incapacity of conviction, and a flinty insensibility to every moral and natural tie, grew of course out of this combination of causes; and men were surely prepared, before themselves were aware, for every plot and perpetration. In these hot beds were sown the seeds of that astonishing Revolution, and all its dreadful appendages, which now spreads dismay and horror throughout half the globe.

While these measures were advancing the great design with a regular and rapid progress, Doctor Adam Weishaupt, professor of the canon law in the University of Ingolstadt, a city of Bavaria (in

Germany) formed, about the year 1777, the order of Illuminati. This order is professedly a higher order of Masons, originated by himself, and grafted on ancient Masonic Institutions. The secrecy, solemnity, mysticism, and correspondence of Masonry, were in this new order preserved and enhanced; while the ardor of innovation, the impatience of civil and moral restraints, and the aims against government, morals, and religion, were elevated, expanded, and rendered more systematical, malignant, and daring.

In the societies of Illuminati doctrines were taught, which strike at the root of all human happiness and virtue; and every such doctrine was either expressly or implicitly involved in their system.

The being of God was denied and ridiculed.

Government was asserted to be a curse, and authority a mere usurpation.

Civil Society was declared to be the only apostasy of man.

The possession of property was pronounced to be robbery.

Chastity and natural affection were declared to be nothing more than groundless prejudices.

Adultery, assassination, poisoning, and other crimes of the like infernal nature, were taught as lawful, and even as virtuous actions.

To crown such a system of falsehood and horror all means were declared to be lawful, provided the end was good.

In this last doctrine men are not only loosed from every bond, and from every duty; but from every inducement to perform anything which is good, and abstain from anything which is evil; and are set upon each other, like a company of hellhounds to worry, rend, and destroy. Of the goodness of the end every man is to judge for himself; and most men, and all men who resemble the Illuminati, will pronounce every end to be good, which will gratify their inclinations. The great and good ends proposed by the Illuminati, as the ultimate objects of their union, are the overthrow of religion, government, and human society civil and domestic. These they pronounce to be so good, that murder, butchery, and war, however extended and dreadful, are declared by them to be completely justifiable, if necessary for these great purposes. With such an example in view, it will be in vain to hunt for ends, which can be evil.

12. Private Diplomacy and Praise for the French: George Logan Denies the Federalist Indictment of Revolutionary France, 16 April 1799.

George Logan of Germantown, Pennsylvania, who was a devout Quaker and an informed advocate of the political and material improvement of mankind, sailed to France in 1798 on a personal mission of peace. Cordially received in Paris by Talleyrand, he secured the release of captured American sailors and a promise that France would now receive negotiators from the United States. Hoping that his mission had contributed to the prospects for peace, Logan returned home, to be execrated by high Federalists and praised by Democratic-Republicans. It is significant that he received the respectful attention of both President John Adams and Charles Cotesworth Pinckney, the South Carolina diplomat who had been rebuffed by the French in 1797 and again at the end of that year in the notorious XYZ affair. A Federalist law of January, 1799, made personal diplomatic missions a federal crime, but although the law remains in effect to this day, no one has ever been convicted under it. George Logan himself broke the law in 1810 when he undertook a peace mission to England. [Copied from *The Mirror*, Washington, Kentucky, 28 June 1799—one of many Democratic-Republican newspapers to carry this public letter. It originally appeared in the Philadelphia *Aurora*.]

To the Citizens of the United States:

The correspondence between Mr. Gerry and the minister of the French Republic, supported by the official communications from Mr. Murray, at the Hague, having removed every doubt on the mind of the President respecting the sincerity of the government of France to preserve a good understanding with the United States, he has appointed a new mission, by which every difficulty between the two republics may be amicably adjusted.

France, from an absolute monarchy, has become a free representative republic; this event alone, is a sufficient cause, with some men, for representing the conduct of the President, in the late appointment, as highly improper: The following observations on the moral and political situation of France, ought to convince unprejudiced minds, that this act of the President is founded in wisdom and sound policy, as with the people from whom the United States may derive greater commercial advantages than from any other nation on earth.

During the last summer, I traveled seven hundred miles through France: The country, everywhere, had the appearance of increasing prosperity: In many places comfortable farm houses were building, and the cottagers, well clothed, exhibited a pleasing appearance of happiness and content.

This numerous, and heretofore degraded class of men, have received immediate advantages from the revolution, whilst the privileged order have been annihilated by its impetuous storms. The cultivators of the earth emancipated from the feudal claims of the nobility—from the monstrous demands of the clergy, and from the personal labor, exacted by unjust laws, for preparing the roads, etc. at this time, form a respectable class of independent citizens, in many instances, living on their own small farms.

The public roads are repairing under a new system of national turnpikes, by the regulations of which, no greater toll is collected than is necessary to preserve the highways in a state of repair. I found traveling perfectly safe, and the expense more reasonable than in the United States.

The municipal officers, established in every part of the Republic, to preserve the public tranquility, are attentive to their functions; and the laws are so highly respected, that although the fields in general are not enclosed, yet the property of a farmer is held sacred; even the extensive gardens in the neighborhood of Paris abounding with the most delicious fruits and vegetables, are free from plunder.

In Paris, the greatest order and regularity exist. The shops are open, and business conducting, as before the revolution. Houses in many parts of the city, [are] building or repairing. The streets [are] regularly lighted and cleansed, and not a beggar or distressed object [is] to be seen.

With respect to religious establishments, the people of France are in opinion with the citizens of the United States. They consider them as foreign to civil institutions. On this account no provision is made, by law, for the support of the clergy of any denomination; nor does the civil law interfere between any man and his Creator; every citizen is left at full liberty to worship God, agreeably to the dictates of his own conscience.

While in Paris, I visited several of the churches, on the Christian sabbath, and was present at the celebration of Mass; the doors of the church being open for the free admission of any person. The same places of worship are, on the day of the Decade, occupied by the Theophilanthropists, a religious sect, something similar in their discipline and manner of worship to the Independents of New England or the Baptists. They commence their worship by prayer, invoking the Supreme Being as the author and fountain of all good, they sing hymns of praise, and conclude their devotions by well-connected sermons on the general principles of morality and virtue; when at the same time they inculcate the duties of every good citizen to maintain the liberties, and to preserve inviolate the laws of his country. In one respect this resembles the Quakers:—every gifted brother has the liberty of preaching without any formal ordination. La Réveillière Lepeaux, President of the Executive Directory, is the patron of this sect.

A foundation of general and universal instruction in the sciences is laid in Paris, which will render that city the first school in Europe for information. The means of knowledge are in such profusion, that it is difficult for a student to make his choice amidst the variety. Public libraries are found in different quarters of the city; the national library, one of the most extensive and best collections of books in the world, is open at all times for the use of the public; tables, paper, ink, etc. are furnished to any person desirous of making extracts from any of the books, which are handed to him by the librarian, attending for that purpose.

The national garden of plants is preserved in complete order, as is also the superb cabinet of natural history; this is the resort of the student, to hear lectures on botany, chemistry, and natural history. The lover of the fine arts will visit, with enthusiasm, the ancient palace of the Louvre, in which are preserved the most exquisite specimens of painting and sculpture from the ancient and modern schools. The national institute enjoys the highest celebrity; its members are divided into classes in such a manner as to procure the greatest quantity of useful information.

I visited the Assembly of Five Hundred and also that of the Ancients. The greatest order and regularity were preserved in all their deliberations.

The Executive Directory has the confidence of the people. Merlin, Lepeaux, and Treilhard, are men of abilities, and attentive to the arduous duties of their office. In private life they are amiable and exemplary citizens. Neufchateau, the minister of the interior, is unremittingly engaged in promoting the internal prosperity of the country, by encouraging agriculture and manufactures. The soil, climate, and local situation of France, will admit these several branches of national wealth to be brought to a great degree of perfection.

The population of France is estimated at thirty-five millions. Her citizens, renovated by the spirit of liberty, and in possession of the heretofore inactive property of the crown and clergy, will render her, in point of finance, the most powerful nation in Europe. Her military establishment, supported by the militia system, in which every citizen is considered as a soldier, and without distinction, is obliged to perform his tour of duty, will preserve the liberties of that country, and, at all times render her formidable.

During an awful moment of revolutionary frenzy, crimes were committed, in violation of the sacred principles of justice and humanity, but these crimes of the revolution have been condemned and punished by the nation. At present no government in Europe is more firmly established, more ably administered, or better calculated to promote the general happiness of its citizens, than that of France.

13. Thomas Jefferson Confronts the French Menace, 18 April 1802.

The war crisis of 1797–8 passed, leaving the ultra-Federalists bereft of the great issue by which they had taken control of national policy. Historians of the United States have praised

President Adams for resisting their efforts to perpetuate the crisis after France had clearly demonstrated a desire for peace. But this was not, as the Democratic-Republicans supposed, a question of our finally clearing up a mere misunderstanding. By 1798, the French Directory had fallen under the influence of its young and brilliant general Napoleon Bonaparte. The ambitious Corsican rejected the idea that a major invasion of Ireland was the best way to destroy British power and launched instead the extraordinary project of controlling the Mediterranean, Egypt, the rest of the Ottoman Empire, and finally the British trading areas of India. Cut off from his supplies by Nelson's victory at the Battle of the Nile, Bonaparte lost a huge army in Egypt. A much smaller force was demolished in Ireland, and the combined force of British and United States armed ships left the French helpless in the western hemisphere. Under these circumstances France needed peace, and offered it on good terms to all her enemies.

Unfortunately for the peace of the world, the sometime enemies of France failed to contain the imperial ambitions of Napoleon, who became First Consul in 1800. He rebuilt his army and navy, forced Spain secretly to "retrocede" Louisiana to France, and prepared a formidable army of invasion and occupation to recapture the French West Indies and rebuild the French Empire in the heart of North America. Jefferson finally learned of Napoleon's scheme early in 1802; his decisive response proves how wrong the ultra-Federalists had been in calling him a tool of France. The following letter is to Robert R. Livingston, United States Minister to France. [Ford, *Writings of Thomas Jefferson* VIII, 144–46.]

. . . The cession of Louisiana and the Floridas by Spain to France works most sorely on the U.S. On this subject the Secretary of State has written to you fully. Yet I cannot forbear recurring to it personally, so deep is the impression it makes in my mind. It completely reverses all the political relations of the U.S. and will form a new epoch in our political course. Of all nations of any consideration France is the one which hitherto has offered the fewest points on which we could have any conflict of right, and the most points of a communion of interests. From these causes we have ever looked to her as our *natural friend,* as one with which we never could have an occasion of difference. Her growth therefore we viewed as our own, her misfortunes ours.

There is on the globe one single spot, the possessor of which is our natural and habitual enemy. It is New Orleans, through which the produce of three-eighths of our territory must pass to market, and from its fertility it will ere long yield more than half of our whole produce and contain more than half our inhabitants. France placing herself in that door assumes to us the attitude of defiance. Spain might have retained it quietly for years. Her pacific dispositions, her feeble state, would induce her to increase our facilities there, so that her possession of the place would be hardly felt by us, and it would not perhaps be very long before some circumstance might arise which might make the cession of it to us the price of something of more worth to her. Not so can it ever be in the hands of France. The impetuosity of her temper, the energy and restlessness of her character, placed in a point of eternal friction with us, and our character, which though quiet, and loving peace and the pursuit of wealth, is high-minded, despising wealth in competition with insult or injury, enterprising and energetic as any nation on earth, these circumstances render it impossible that France and the U.S. can continue long friends when they meet in so irritable a position. They as well as we must be blind if they do not see this; and we must be very improvident if we do not begin to make arrangements on that hypothesis. The day that France takes possession of New Orleans fixes the sentence which is to restrain her forever within her low water mark. It seals the union of two nations who in conjunction can maintain exclusive possession of the ocean. From that moment we must marry ourselves to the British fleet and nation. We must turn all our attentions to a maritime force, for which our resources place us on very high grounds: and having formed and cemented together a power which may render reinforcement of her settlements here impossible to France, make the first cannon, which shall be fired in Europe, the signal for tearing up any settlement she may have made, and for holding the two continents of America in sequestration for the common purposes of the united British and American nations.

This is not a state of things we seek or desire. It is one which this measure, if adopted by France, forces on us, as necessarily as any other cause, by the laws of nature, brings on its necessary effect. It is not from a fear of France that we deprecate this measure proposed by her. For however greater her force is than ours compared in the abstract, it is nothing in comparison of ours when to be exerted on our soil. But it is from a sincere love of peace, and a firm persuasion that bound to France by the interests and the strong sympathies still existing in the minds of our citizens, and holding relative positions which ensure their continuance we are secure of a long course of peace. Whereas the change of friends, which will be rendered necessary if France changes that position, embarks us necessarily as a belligerent power in the first war of Europe. In that case France will have held possession of New Orleans during the interval of a peace, long or short, at the end of which it will be wrested from her. Will this short-lived possession have been an equivalent to her for the transfer of such a weight into the scale of her enemy? Will not the amalgamation of a young, thriving nation continue to that enemy the health and force which are at present so evidently on the decline? And will a few years possession of New Orleans add equally to the strength of France?

She may say she needs Louisiana for the supply of her West Indies. She does not need it in time of peace. And in war she could not depend on them because they would be so easily intercepted. I should suppose that all these considerations might in some proper form be brought into view of the government of France. Though stated by us, it ought not to give offense, because we do not bring them forward as a menace, but as consequences not controllable by us, but inevitable from the course of things. We mention them not as things which we desire by any means, but as things we deprecate; and we beseech a friend to look forward and to prevent them for our common interests.

If France considers Louisiana however as indispensable for her views she might perhaps be willing to look about for arrangements which might reconcile it to our interests. If anything could do this it would be the ceding to us the island of New Orleans and the Floridas. This would certainly in a great degree remove the causes of jarring and irritation between us, and perhaps for such a length of time as might produce other means of making the measure permanently conciliatory to our interests and friendships. It would at any rate relieve us from the necessity of taking immediate measures for countervailing such an operation by arrangements in another quarter. . . .

14. Thomas Jefferson's Indian Policy, 27 February 1803.

The following letter to William Henry Harrison, Governor of the Indiana Territory, contains a full exposition of Jefferson's plans for the future of the American Indian. The special urgency of the letter reflects Jefferson's concern over the Louisiana crisis, not yet resolved. [Clarence Edwin Carter, *The Territorial Papers of the United States* VII; (Washington, D. C., 1939), VII 89–92.]

. . . From the Secretary at War you receive from time to time information and instructions as to our Indian affairs. These communications being for the public records are restrained always to particular objects and occasions. But this letter being unofficial, and private, I may with safety give you a more extensive view of our policy respecting the Indians, that you may the better comprehend the parts dealt out to you in detail through the official channel, and observing the system of which they make a part, conduct yourself in unison with it in cases where you are obliged to act without instruction. Our system is to live in perpetual peace with the Indians, to cultivate an affectionate attachment from them, by everything just and liberal which we can [do] for them within the bounds of reason, and by giving them effectual protection against wrongs from our own people. The decrease of game rendering their subsistence by hunting insufficient, we wish to draw them to agriculture, to spinning and weaving. The latter branches they take up with great readiness, because they fall to the women, who gain by quitting the labors of the field for these which are exercised within doors. When they withdraw themselves to the culture of a small piece of land, they will perceive how useless to them are their extensive forests, and will be willing to pare them off from time to time in exchange for necessaries for their farms and families.

To promote this disposition to exchange lands, which they have to spare and we want, for necessaries, which we have to spare and they want, we shall push our trading houses, and be glad to see the good and influential individuals among them run in debt, because we observe that when these debts get beyond what the individuals can pay, they become willing to lop [them off] by a cession of lands. At our trading houses too we mean to sell so low as merely to repay us cost and charges so as neither to lessen or enlarge our capital. This is what private traders cannot do, for they must gain; they will consequently retire from the competition, and we shall thus get clear of this pest without giving offense or umbrage to the Indians. In this way our settlements will gradually circumscribe and approach the Indians, and they will in time either incorporate with us as citizens of the U.S. or remove beyond the Mississippi. The former is certainly the termination of their history most happy for themselves. But in the whole course of this, it is essential to cultivate their love. As to their fear, we presume that our strength and their weakness is now so visible that they must see we have only to shut our hand to crush them, and that all our liberalities to them proceed from motives of pure humanity only. Should any tribe be foolhardy enough to take up the hatchet at any time, the seizing the whole country of that tribe and driving them across the Mississippi, as the only condition of peace, would be an example to others, and a furtherance of our final consolidation.

Combined with these views and to be prepared against the occupation of Louisiana by a powerful and enterprising people, it is important that setting less value on interior extension of purchases from the Indians, we bend our whole views to the purchase and settlement of the country on the Mississippi from its mouth to its northern regions, that we may be able to present as strong a front on our western as on our eastern border, and plant on the Mississippi itself the means of its own defence. We now own from 31° to the Yazoo, and hope this summer to purchase what belongs to the Choctaws from the Yazoo up to their boundary, supposed to be about opposite the mouth of Acanza. We wish at the same time to begin in your quarter, for which there is at present a favorable opening. The Cahokias being extinct, we are entitled to their country by our paramount sovereignty. The Peorias we understand have all been driven off from their country, and we might claim it in the same way; but as we understand there is one chief remaining, who would, as the survivor of the tribe, sell the right, it will be better to give him such terms as will make him easy for life, and take a conveyance from him. The Kaskaskias being reduced to a few families, I presume we may purchase their whole country for what would place every individual of them at his ease, and be a small price to us, say by laying off for each family wherever they would choose it as much rich land as they could cultivate, adjacent to each other, inclosing the whole in a single fence, and giving them such an annuity in money or goods forever as would place them in happiness. And we might take them also under the protection of the U.S.

Thus possessed of the rights of these three tribes, we should proceed to the settling their boundaries with the Pottawatomies and Kickapoos, claiming all doubtful territory, but paying them a price for the relinquishment of their concurrent claim, and even prevailing on them if possible to cede for a price such of their own unquestioned territory as would give us a convenient northern boundary. Before broaching this, and while we are bargaining with the Kaskaskias, the minds of the Pottawatomies and Kickapoos should be soothed and conciliated by liberalities and sincere assurances of friendship. Perhaps by sending a well-qualified character to stay some time in Decoigne's village as if on other business, and to sound him and introduce the subject by degrees to his mind and that of the other heads of families, inculcating in the way of conversation all those considerations which prove the advantages they would receive by a cession on those terms, the object might be more easily and effectually obtained than by abruptly proposing it to them at a formal treaty. Of the means however of obtaining what we wish you will be the best judge, and I have given you this view of the system which we suppose will best promote the interests of the Indians and ourselves, and finally consolidate our whole country into one nation only, that you may be enabled the better to adapt your means to the object. For these purposes we have given you a general commission for treating.

The crisis is pressing. Whatever can now be obtained, must be obtained quickly. The occupation of New Orleans, hourly expected, by the French, is already felt like a light breeze by the Indians. You know the sentiments they entertain of that nation. Under the hope of their protection, they will immediately stiffen against cessions of land to us. We had better therefore do at once what can now be done.

I must repeat that this letter is to be considered as private and friendly. It is not to contradict any particular instructions which you may receive through the official channel. You will also perceive how sacredly it must be kept within [your] own breast, and especially how improper to be understood by the Indians. [In] their interests and their tranquility it is best they should see only the present [page] of their history. I pray you to accept assurances [of] my esteem and high consideration. . . .

15. Timothy Pickering
Considering Disunion,
29 January 1804.

Napoleon's splendid army never reached New Orleans, for it was destroyed by tropical diseases and the black inhabitants of Santo Domingo. This and the resumption of war in Europe caused Napoleon to sell Louisiana to the United States before Jefferson made good his threat to ally with the British and take it by force. Most Americans rejoiced in the Louisiana Purchase, but a few recalcitrant Federalists saw in it nothing but the infinite extension of the southern planting economy, which they regarded as the economic base of Democratic-Republican politics. Rather than admire the remarkable addition to the nation's wealth and security, such Federalists imagined that they would be certainly the victims of increasing tyranny. Timothy Pickering explained the situation to George Cabot of Boston in the following letter. [Henry Cabot Lodge, *The Life and Letters of George Cabot* (Boston, 1878), pp. 337–40.]

My Dear Sir,   A friend of mine in Pennsylvania, in answering a letter, lately asked me, "Is not a great deal of our chagrin founded on personal dislikes, the pride of opinion, and the mortification of disappointment?" I replied, or to speak correctly, I prepared the following reply. But when I had finished, perceiving the sentiments too strong for the latitude of Pennsylvania, and perhaps for the nerves of my friend, I changed the form, and now address them to you.

To those questions, perhaps to a certain degree, an affirmative answer may be given. I have more than once asked myself, for what are we struggling? Our lands yield their increase, our commerce flourishes, we are building houses, "are marrying and given in marriage," yet we are dissatisfied, not because we envy the men in office—to most of us a private life is of the most desirable. The Federalists are dissatisfied because they see the public morals debased by the corrupt and corrupting system of our rulers. Men are tempted to become apostates, not to Federalism merely, but to virtue and to religion, and to good government. Apostasy and original depravity are the qualifications for official honors and emoluments, while men of sterling worth are displaced and held up to popular contempt and scorn. And shall we sit still, until this system shall universally triumph? . . .

My life is not worth much, but, if it must be offered up, let it rather be in the hope of obtaining a more stable government, under which my children, at least, may enjoy freedom with security. Some Connecticut gentlemen (and they are well informed and discreet) assure me that, if the leading Democrats in that State were to get the upper hand (which would be followed by a radical change in their *unwritten* constitution), they should not think themselves safe, either in person or property, and would therefore immediately quit the state. I do not believe in the practicability of a long-continued union. A northern confederacy would unite congenial characters, and present a fairer prospect of public happiness; while the southern states, having a similarity of habits, might be left "to manage their own affairs in their own way." If a separation were to take place, our mutual wants would render a friendly and commercial intercourse inevitable. The southern states would require the naval protection of the northern union, and the products of the former would be important to the navigation and commerce of the latter. I believe, indeed, that, if a northern confederacy were forming, our southern brethren would be seriously alarmed, and probably abandon their virulent measures. But I greatly doubt whether prudence should suffer the connection to continue much longer . . .

But *when* and *how* is a separation to be effected? If, as many think, Federalism (by which I mean the solid principles of government applied to a federate republic,—principles which are founded in justice, in sound morals, and religion, and whose object is the security of life, liberty, and property against popular delusion, injustice, and tyranny); if, I say, Federalism is crumbling away in New England, there is no time to be lost, lest it should be overwhelmed, and become unable to attempt its own relief. Its last refuge is New England, and immediate exertion, perhaps, its only hope. It must begin in Massachusetts. The proposition would be welcomed in Connecticut, and could we doubt of New Hampshire? But New York must be associated, and how is her concurrence to be obtained? She must be made the center of the confederacy. Vermont and New Jersey would follow of course, and Rhode Island of necessity. Who can be consulted, and who will take the lead? The legislatures of Massachusetts and Connecticut meet in May and of New Hampshire in the same month or in June. The subject has engaged the contemplation of many. The Connecticut gentlemen have seriously meditated upon it.

We suppose the British provinces in Canada and Nova Scotia, at no remote period, perhaps without delay, and with the assent of Great Britain, may become members of the northern league. Certainly that government can feel only disgust at our present rulers. She will be pleased to see them crestfallen. She will not regret the proposed division of empire. If with their own consent she relinquishes her provinces, she will be rid of the charge of maintaining them, while she will derive from *them*, as she does from *us*, all the commercial returns which her merchants now receive. A liberal treaty of amity and commerce will form a bond of union between Great Britain and the northern confederacy highly useful to both. . . .

16. Jefferson's Pursuit of Florida, 12 November 1805.

After concluding the triumph of the Louisiana Purchase, James Monroe went on to Madrid with instructions from Jefferson and Madison to purchase East and West Florida. The United States had already put forward a claim to part of West Florida that was based on its having once been part of Louisiana. The Spanish refused Monroe's advances, and the French now supported their ally. Jefferson's response to this situation was similar to that of 1802. He contemplated an alliance with Britain that would permit us to seize the Floridas with ease and safety. Toward the end of 1805, the spread of war in Europe suggested a better method, which is sketched in the following memorandum of a cabinet meeting. [Ford, *Writings of Thomas Jefferson*, I, 308.]

Present the four secretaries, subject Spanish affairs. The extension of the war in Europe leaving us without danger of a sudden peace, depriving us of the chance of an ally, I proposed we should address ourselves to France, informing her it was a last effort at amicable settlement with Spain, and offer to her or through her, 1. A sum of money for the rights of Spain east of Iberville, say the Floridas. 2. To cede the part of Louisiana from the Rio Bravo to the Guadelupe. 3. Spain to pay within a certain time spoliations under her own flag agreed to by the convention (which we guess to be 100 vessels worth 2 million) and those subsequent (worth as much more) and to hypothecate to us for those payments the country from Guadelupe to Rio Bravo. Armstrong to be employed. The first was to be the exciting motive with France to whom Spain is in arrears for subsidies and who will be glad also to secure us from going into the scale of England. The second the soothing motive with Spain which France would press bona fide because she claimed to the Rio Bravo. The third to quiet our merchants. It was agreed to unanimously and the sum to be offered fixed not to exceed 5 million dollars. Mr.

Gallatin did not like purchasing Florida under an apprehension of war, lest we should be thought in fact to purchase peace. We thought this overweighed by taking advantage of an opportunity which might not occur again of getting a country essential to our peace, and to the security of the commerce of the Mississippi. . . .

III

Crisis, War, and Peace
with Britain, 1805–1815

1. Britain's Growing Annoyance
with the United States, 1805.

Thomas Jefferson often was accused of being excessively pro-French and anti-British. The French diplomat Pierre Adet knew better. He wrote to his government on 31 December 1796 that "Jefferson, I say, is American and, as such, he cannot be sincerely our friend. An American is the born enemy of all the European peoples." [Translated from the French by Dumas Malone, *Jefferson and the Ordeal of Liberty;* Boston, 1962; 289–90.] Jefferson had believed in the 1790's that the British were, as they had been in the 1770's, the great menace to American freedom and growth and that the French alliance satisfactorily offset British power. But as President, Jefferson inherited the cordial relations that had grown up between Britain and the United States during the Adams administration. Seeing our trade flourish and our territory widen, Jefferson was entirely happy and was even willing to involve the United States further with Britain in order to counteract Napoleon's threat of 1802–3 or to assist our aggrandizement from Spanish territory. But the spread of warfare in Europe brought back the unpleasant situation of 1793. The French once more diverted much of their imperial trade to American shipping, which had been able, under the *Polly* decision in the British courts, to circumvent the Rule of 1756 by carrying French cargoes to the United States before continuing with

them to Europe. But that was 1800, after the United States
had in effect helped Britain win a naval war against France.
By 1805, the United States once more was helping the French,
in effect, to evade British blockades. Sir William Scott, the
English judge who had pronounced in the *Polly* case, now
reversed himself, in the *Essex* case, and without warning,
British cruisers began seizing American ships. This was not a
case of a single jurist changing the course of history. A seg-
ment of the British public had taken offense at the astonishing growth and prosperity of the United States. In this instance, we have not a report from an eyewitness authority,
but a classic statement, by Henry Adams, of the change in
British feeling. [*History of the United States of America During the Second Administration of Thomas Jefferson* (New
York, 1903), I, 50–53.]

. . . All the interested classes of England, except the manufacturers
and merchants who were concerned in commerce with the United
States, agreed in calling upon government to crush out the neutral
trade. Sir William Scott had merely required an additional proof
of its honesty; England with one voice demanded that, honest or
not, it should be stopped.

This almost universal prayer found expression in a famous pamphlet that has rarely had an equal for ability and effect. In October, 1805, three months after the "Essex" decision, while Monroe
was advising Madison to press harder than ever on all the great
belligerent Powers, appeared in London a book of more than two
hundred pages, with the title: *War in Disguise; or, the Frauds of
the Neutral Flags.* The author was James Stephen, a man not less
remarkable for his own qualities than for those which two genera-
tions of descendants have inherited from him; but these abilities,
though elevating him immensely above the herd of writers who in
England bespattered America with abuse, and in America befouled
England, were yet of a character so peculiar as to bar his path to
the highest distinction. James Stephen was a high-minded fanatic,
passionately convinced of the truths he proclaimed. Two years after
writing *War in Disguise,* he published another pamphlet, maintaining that the Napoleonic wars were a divine chastisement of England

for her tolerance of the slave-trade; and this curious thesis he argued through twenty pages of close reasoning. Through life a vehement enemy of slavery, at a time when England rang with abuse of America, which he had done much to stimulate, he had the honesty and courage to hold America up as an example before Europe, and to assert that in abolishing the slave-trade she had done an act for which it was impossible to refuse her the esteem of England, and in consequence of which he prayed that harmony between the two countries might be settled on the firmest foundation.

This insular and honest dogmatism, characteristic of many robust minds, Stephen carried into the question of neutral trade. He had himself begun his career in the West Indies, and in the prize-court at St. Kitt's had learned the secrets of neutral commerce. Deeply impressed with the injury which this trade caused to England, he believed himself bound to point out the evil and the remedy to the British public. Assuming at the outset that the Rule of 1756 was a settled principle of law, he next assumed that the greater part of the neutral trade was not neutral at all, but was a fraudulent business, in which French or Spanish property, carried in French or Spanish ships, was by means of systematic perjury protected by the prostituted American flag.

How much of this charge was true will never be certainly known. Stephen could not prove his assertions. The American merchants stoutly denied them. Alexander Baring, better informed than Stephen and far less prejudiced, affirmed that the charge was untrue, and that if the facts could be learned, more British than enemy's property would be found afloat under the American flag. Perhaps this assertion was the more annoying of the two; but to prove either the one or the other was needless, since from such premises Stephen was able to draw a number of startling conclusions which an English public stood ready to accept. The most serious of these was the certain ruin of England from the seduction of her seamen into this fraudulent service; another was the inevitable decay of her merchant marine; still another pointed to the loss of the Continental market; and he heightened the effect of all these evils by adding a picture of the British admiral in the decline of life raised to the peerage for his illustrious actions, and enjoying a pension from the national bounty, but still unable to spend so much money as became an English peer, because his Government had denied to him the "safe booty" of the neutral trade! . . .

Thus a conviction was established in England that the American trade was a fraud which must soon bring Great Britain to ruin, and that the Americans who carried on this commerce were carrying on a "war in disguise" for the purpose of rescuing France and Spain from the pressure of the British navy. The conclusion was inevitable. "Enforce the Rule of 1756!" cried Stephen; "cut off the neutral trade altogether!" This policy, which went far beyond the measures of Pitt and the decision of Sir William Scott, was urged by Stephen with great force; while he begged the Americans, in temperate and reasonable language, not to make war for the protection of so gross a fraud. Other writers used no such self-restraint. The austere and almost religious conviction of Stephen could maintain itself at a height where no personal animosity toward America mingled its bitterness with his denunciations; but his followers, less accustomed than he to looking for motives in their Bibles, said simply that the moment for going to war with the United States had come, and that the opportunity should be seized. . . .

2. Anthony Merry Promoting the Project of Aaron Burr, 29 March 1805.

Some authorities still doubt that Aaron Burr seriously intended to split off the western part of the United States. If the following letter does not prove Burr's treasonous designs, it surely establishes that Anthony Merry, the British minister to the United States, enjoyed the prospect of a division and weakening of this country. Pitt's government wisely declined to involve itself with Burr. But the British absorbed the dangerous notion that the West was discontented and might be separated from the United States by a timely stroke. [Merry to Harrowby, No. 15. Henry Adams Transcripts, Library of Congress.]

Most Secret

My Lord, Notwithstanding the known profligacy of Mr. Burr's character I am encouraged to report to Your Lordship the substance of some secret communications which he has sought occasion to make to me since he has been out of office, (by the circumstances which I had the honor to state in a preceding dispatch of this date) of the disaffection manifested by the deputies [from Louisiana] at the conduct of this government and of the sentiments which they express on the occasion to persons in whom they consider that they might place a confidence and which they also conveyed to me, although not in so explicit a manner, in some conversations I have had with them.

Mr. Burr, with whom I know that the deputies became very intimate during their residence here, has mentioned to me that the inhabitants of Louisiana seem determined to render themselves independent of the United States and that the execution of their design is only delayed by the difficulty of obtaining previously an assurance of protection and assistance from some foreign power and of concerting and connecting their independence with that of the inhabitants of the western parts of the United States, who must always have a command over them by the rivers which communicate with the Mississippi.

It is clear that Mr. Burr (although he has not yet confided to me the exact nature and extent of his plan) means to endeavor to be the instrument for effecting such a connection. He has told me that the inhabitants of Louisiana, notwithstanding that they are almost all of French or Spanish origin, as well as those of the western part of the United States, would, for many obvious reasons, prefer having the protection and assistance of Great Britain to the support of France, but that if His Majesty's Government should not think proper to listen to this overture, application will be made to that of France, who will, he had reason to know, be eager to attend to it in the most effectual manner, observing, that peace in Europe would accelerate the event in question by affording to the French more easy means of communication with the continent of America, though, even while at war with England, they might always find those of sending the small force that would be required for the purpose in question.

He pointed out the great commercial advantage which His Majesty's Dominions in general would derive from furnishing almost exclusively (as they might do through Canada and New Orleans) the inhabitants of so extensive a territory, where the population is increased with astonishing rapidity, with every article necessary for their consumption, while the impossibility of the country in question ever becoming a naval power (since it would have only one bad port, that of New Oreans, where no large vessels can pass) and, consequently, of any jealousy or ill will arising from that cause, would ensure the permanent and beneficial intercourse above mentioned.

Mr. Burr observed that it would be too dangerous and even premature to disclose to me at present, the full extent and detail of the plan he had formed, but that he was at the same time aware of the necessity of making the most ample and unreserved communication to His Majesty's Government, in order that they might be fully satisfied, as well of the good faith with which he means to act, as of the practicability and utility to them, of the undertaking which he had in view and that he would therefore send a confidential person to England to make those communications as soon as he should have received, through me, the necessary assurance of their being disposed to grant the protection and assistance required to accomplish the object.

In regard to military aid he said two or three frigates and the same number of smaller vessels to be stationed at the mouth of the Mississippi to prevent its being blockaded by such force as the United States could send, and to keep open the communication with the sea would be the whole that would be wanted; and in respect to money the loan of about one hundred thousand pounds, would, he conceived, be sufficient for the immediate purposes of the enterprise, although it was impossible for him to speak at present with accuracy as to this matter. On the latter allegation he observed that any suspicion of His Majesty's Government being concerned in the transaction, till after their independence should have been declared, which would arise if remittances were made to this country or if bills were drawn from hence, might be avoided by the appropriation to this object of a proportion of the two hundred thousand pounds which the United States have to pay His Majesty next July, any part of which sum, he would devise the means to get into his possession without its destination being either known or suspected.

Should the object in question be considered worth the attention of the British Government, he begs leave to recommend to them to lose no time in sending out an intelligent and confidential person as consul, to New Orleans, observing that it would be proper that he should possess the French language. Mr. Burr concluded by saying that he would adopt safe means to inform me, whenever his plan should be brought to maturity, and by requesting that His Majesty's Ministers would be pleased to communicate their disposition to afford the protection and assistance solicited, with as little delay as the consideration of so important a matter might require. He explained to me the reason of his being, apparently, on so cordial a footing with the government here during the late session of Congress, though I cannot but suspect that he has been disappointed in his views. I have only to add that if a strict confidence could be placed in him, he certainly possesses perhaps in a much greater degree than any other individual in this country, all the talents, energy, intrepidity and firmness which are requisite for such an enterprise. At all events I have thought it to be my duty to make Your Lordship acquainted with his proposition. . . .

3. Merry Finds Madison Quarrelsome, 30 June 1805.

Two British warships, the *Cambrian* and the *Leander*, had stationed themselves outside New York harbor in the summer of 1804, originally at the request of American merchants suffering from French privateers lurking in the vicinity. The cure proved worse than the disease, for under the direction of the aggressive Captain Bradley of the *Cambrian*, a press gang boarded a British merchantman and carried off twenty sailors right in New York harbor, grossly violating American jurisdiction. Worse, the British ships began stopping and searching American merchantmen sailing from New York, seeking French contraband and deserters from the British Navy. The British accepted American protests and recalled Captain Bradley. That might have ended the matter, for Jefferson then hopefully believed that good relations could be maintained with Britain. When violations of our neutrality increased and Madison learned that Captain Bradley had in fact been promoted, the old *Cambrian* case lived on and on as one of those annoyances that, in final great accumulation, drove the United States to declare war. The very tediousness of Merry's letter to his new superior, Lord Mulgrave, is instructive in showing the Englishman's impatience with American presumption and the distressing combination of prolixity and nagging that marked the diplomacy of the Secretary of State, James Madison. [Henry Adams Transcripts, Library of Congress.]

My Lord, I have the honor to transmit to Your Lordship enclosed copies of a communication, and of the papers referred to in it, which the American Secretary of State has made to me of the instructions which the President has at length caused to be issued in consequence of the act passed in the last session of Congress for the more effectual preservation of peace in the ports and harbors of the United States. . . .

On the occasion of my seeing the Secretary of State a few days ago at his office, he said that he would take that opportunity of mentioning to me the very great sensation which the news, lately arrived, of Captain Bradley's having been appointed to the command of a ship of the line had produced in the mind of the President and of this government in general. He observed that the circumstance of His Majesty's Government having upon the first report which had reached them of that officer's proceedings in the Port of New York last year thought proper to deprive him of the command of the *Cambrian* frigate, and to recall him for the purpose of making an inquiry into his conduct, seemed to show that the impropriety of it must have been evident to them from the first moment, and that, as it could only have been confirmed by the statements and documents which he had transmitted to me, they had every reason to flatter themselves that the satisfaction for it which they had demanded would have been granted by Captain Bradley experiencing some further mark of His Majesty's displeasure. Instead of this, if the proposed inquiry had in fact taken place, it was to be inferred from that officer's promotion, instead of his punishment, having been the result of it, that his conduct had rather been approved than otherwise, which would afford encouragement not only to him but to every other officer in the British Navy to repeat, what he termed the same insults and excesses in the ports of the United States.

He remarked that so unexpected a determination on the part of His Majesty's Government had been lamented greatly by the President, and that it could not fail to produce the most unfavorable effect throughout this country, adding, that although the particular instructions which had been sent on this head to Mr. Monroe had not reached that minister before his departure for Spain, and did not appear to have been acted upon by the Chargé d'Affaires in London, it had been hoped that the representations made to me might have been sufficient to have ensured to this government that satisfaction to which they could not but consider themselves justly entitled. In my reply to Mr. Madison I observed to him, that he might recollect that in the correspondence which I had the honor to have with him respecting the transaction to which he now alluded, it had not been in my power to agree with him as to the charges brought against Captain Bradley in the full extent to which he had been pleased to carry them; that His Majesty's Government had given a most unequivocal proof of their earnest disposition to give every satisfaction to the United States that the nature of the case might appear to them to require by not waiting for any representations on their part before they removed Captain Bradley from the command of the frigate, and directed him to return to England, to account for his proceedings; that this very determination not only marked a disapprobation of his conduct, but was in fact a serious punishment for it, that officer having suffered a disgrace by it, and having moreover during the time of his suspension lost all the advantages which attend actual service; that the command which was said to have been since given to him of a ship of the line ought not to be regarded as a promotion, or even as a mark of any favor, since I had reason to believe, from what I had frequently heard the officers of His Majesty's Navy express on the subject, that they considered the command of a large fast-sailing frigate, such as the

Cambrian was, as the most eligible of any they could obtain; and that, for the rest, I had received no official information of what had, in fact, been the result of the inquiry made into Captain Bradley's conduct. I have to regret, My Lord, that these observations were not sufficient to do away in any degree the idea with which the American Secretary of State was so strongly impressed that His Majesty's Government had been wanting in a proper attention to the complaints made from hence, for he contended that the command of a ship of the line was a trust superior to that of a frigate, and that such an appointment in favor of Captain Bradley could not but be considered as an advancement to him in the line of his service; that if his removal from the Cambrian, and his recall to England had been, as I had endeavored to show it to be, any punishment at all, it was by no means adequate to the nature of his offense, and of course not such a satisfaction as the United States had a right to expect; and he concluded by saying, that since Mr. Monroe had not had an opportunity of carrying into execution the first instructions which had been sent to him on this head, the circumstance of what he still called Captain Bradley's promotion, would now render it necessary for fresh directions to be given to that minister to make proper representations respecting it to His Majesty's Government, and that he had therefore thought it proper to make me acquainted with the President's sentiments in regard to this subject. Such having been the result of my conversation with Mr. Madison, I have deemed it necessary to trouble Your Lordship with this detail of it. . . .

4. The Santo Domingo Embargo, 20 February 1806.

Napoleon had given up on Louisiana, but he remained determined to regain control of the valuable sugar colony of Santo Domingo, or what is now known as Haiti. The Negro rebels on that island enjoyed with the United States a mutually profitable trade that was entirely illegal from the French point of view. Napoleon directed Talleyrand to inform the United States government that this trade must cease, that its continuance could only be viewed as hostility to France. Ever since Nelson's brilliant victory at Trafalgar in October, 1805, the Emperor had concentrated upon European land campaigns; so there were no direct means by which he could challenge the United States-Santo Domingo trade. But in 1806, Jefferson still was hoping to use French pressure to pry the Floridas from Spain. This maneuver had to be kept secret; so the Santo Domingo Embargo Bill appeared before the Senate and the House merely as something the United States ought to enact out of respect to the sovereignty of a friendly nation.

There was little debate in either branch of Congress. A few Federalists barely hinted that the United States ought to resist European efforts to reconquer former colonies. This aroused several Southern members to denounce the Negroes of Santo Domingo and even to express the fear that continued independence there might foment slave insurrections in the United States. There was only one major speech on the Santo Domingo embargo, by Samuel White, the moderate Federalist Senator from Delaware. John Quincy Adams, then a Senator from Massachusetts, called it "one of the most powerful and beautiful speeches I have ever heard made in Congress." [Memoirs, (Philadelphia, 1874), I, 414.] Adams undoubtedly was moved by the clarity with which White foresaw the expansion of United States economic power. Though critics of the bill easily won what passed for debate, it was enacted by large majorities in both Houses. Southerners voted for it as a measure against the rebel Negroes, and Democratic-Republicans from other sections voted out of party loyalty. Federalists and a few maverick Democratic-Republicans opposed it because they disliked Napoleon and disliked restrictions on American trade. The following is from the speech of Senator White. [Annals of Congress (9th Congress, 1st Session), pp. 118–24, 131–33.]

. . . Neither in justice nor in wisdom, sir, is it the duty or the interest of this Government to adopt the present measure. I do not, as some other gentlemen have professed, consider it a measure of policy, nor will I call it a measure of fear; but it certainly savors of the most timid prudence I have ever seen operating in this body, little calculated to acquire us honor abroad, or to prolong our peace at home; and if gentlemen have really persuaded themselves that the decision we are about to make involves merely a question of policy, in my humble opinion they most egregiously mistake. No such construction will be given to it; none such, give me leave to say, is it entitled to bear. The surrender of this commerce has never been asked of us as a temporary sacrifice to the convenience and accommodation of France; but has been demanded of us, in the most insulting and peremptory style, as a matter of right; and passing this bill, under present circumstances, will be an acknowledgment of the right in France to interdict us this trade. It will be a direct abandonment of all right to it on our part, and establishing a precedent against ourselves, that will be held obligatory upon us in all future cases of the same kind. In this aspect the subject must develop itself to every gentleman as one of the utmost magnitude to the United States. If our commerce with Santo Domingo was worth nothing, I would equally resist the present measure; it is the principle I object to. I object, and will forever object, to the solemn recognition on the part of this Government, of a right in foreign powers that may, and hereafter will be exercised, if now admitted, to the injury of the American commerce, and of the American character. If gentlemen will look for a moment about them, will attend to our position in the world, and to the colonial establishments of the European nations around us, they cannot but be convinced, that cases similar to this must often happen. The sooner we take our ground, therefore, the better; the less difficulty we shall have hereafter; and surely a more suitable opportunity than the present can never be expected to occur; especially, sir, when we reflect upon the most uncourtly, indignant, and domineering manner, by which France has attempted to bully and terrify us into this measure of the gentleman from Pennsylvania—and the gentleman himself, yesterday, unmasked the bill. In his great zeal he told us that we had already tampered too long on the subject; that France had now demanded the measure of us, and its adoption had become a matter of necessity on our part. Degrading idea! Where then has gone our national honor and our boasted independence? What was this but to tell us, that such is now our humbled state, when France commands we have no alternative but obedience; and that even to deliberate is dangerous? [Here Mr. Logan observed that he did not recollect having used the word "demanded;" to which another gentleman answered, he certainly had.]

I had expected, Mr. President, as must have been the case with every other gentleman, that the honorable mover of this measure, (Mr. L.) when he submitted to the Senate a proposition of such infinite importance, would have assigned at least some plausible reasons for doing so; but we are now as much in the dark as when our attention was first called to the subject . . .

I will here cursorily premise, that I must be excused in passing over, without observation, the communications that have been recently made on this subject by the French Minister to our Government, and by Mr. Talleyrand to General Armstrong. They are of a kind not to admit of comments, without provoking such animadversions as the respect due to the exalted stations those gentlemen fill, and to the Government they represent, will not permit me to indulge myself in for a moment. One thing, however, I will say: that whatever influence their threats and invectives may acquire, certainly their arguments are entitled to none; for they have not condescended to use a single one; but have taken as granted the very points in dispute, viz: that the blacks of Santo Domingo are the slaves of the French, and now in such a state of revolt that no nation has a right to trade with them. To these points I will presently give some attention, after a few observations on the subject of our West India commerce, generally, as connected with this question.

It is well known, sir, that a considerable portion of the commerce, which of late years has so rapidly enriched our citizens, and advanced, beyond the most sanguine calculations, our national wealth and political consequence, has consisted in the increased intercourse with the West India islands; and this has arisen chiefly from our neutral and neighboring situation toward those islands: from the unrestrained and enterprising spirit of our merchants, and from a combination of circumstances that have been sufficient to involve, and continue in war for a number of years, the most commercial powers of Europe. So extensive and valuable has our trade become in the West Indian seas, that it has excited, and is daily increasing the jealousies of other nations; and, certainly, in the same gradation, at least, should increase our disposition to protect and to foster it. But what, let me ask, must be the inevitable operation of the measure now before us? To prostrate completely, at a single blow, the most valuable part of it remaining, and to jeopardize the whole. As if not content with the branches that have been lopped off by the British, the French, and the Spaniards, the gentleman from Pennsylvania will himself now lay the axe to the root of the tree; and this, too, at a moment when our commerce is approaching the most crippled and ruinous condition; when the principal commercial nations of Europe are exerting every effort short of actual war to crush it; when your table is loaded with the memorials of your citizens, complaining of the injustice and violence to which they are subjected in every part of the world, and praying the protection of their government; when the President of the United States is communicating to us message after message upon this very subject; when almost every mail that arrives brings to us the unwelcome intelligence of some additional outrages upon the persons and the property of our countrymen; and scarcely a wind from any quarter of the globe but swells the catalogue of their grievances.

Our local situation, Mr. President, gives to us advantages in the commerce of the West Indies over all the nations of the world; and it is not only the right and the interest, but it is the duty of this government, by every fair and honorable means, to protect and encourage our citizens in the exercise of those advantages. If, in other respects, we pursue a wise policy, and remain abstracted from the convulsions of Europe, that for many years to come are not likely to have much interval; enjoying, as we shall, all the advantages of peace-wages, peace-freight, peace-insurance, and the other peace privileges of neutral traders, we must nearly acquire a monopoly of this commerce. We can make usually a treble voyage; that is, from this continent to the West Indies, thence to Europe, and back to America again, in the time that the European vessels are engaged in one West India voyage. This circumstance of itself, properly improved, at a period perhaps not very remote, whenever others of those islands may be released from, or refuse longer submission to their present colonial restrictions upon commerce, will enable us to rival even the British in transporting to the markets of Europe the very valuable productions of the West Indies, such as sugar, molasses, coffee, spirits, etc. Again, sir, I state nothing new when I say that the produce of this country is essential to the West India islands, and the facility with which we can convey it to them, must at all times enable us to furnish them much cheaper than they can be furnished by any other people. It requires not indeed the spirit of prophecy to foretell, that the time must come when the very convenient and commanding situation we occupy, in every point of view, relative to the most valuable of those islands, will place in our hands the entire control of their trade . . .

I will now, sir, notice the relative hostile situations of France and Santo Domingo, and see how far gentlemen are borne out in their positions—that the people of Santo Domingo can be considered only as revolted slaves, or, at best, as French subjects now in a state of rebellion; that they are nationally in no respect separated from France; that to trade with them is a violation of the laws of nations, and that we have no right to do so. This, so far as I could understand them, forms a summary of the points that have been urged in support of the present measure, and in opposition to the trade; each of which deserves some attention. If I am wrong in these points, the friends of the bill will please now to correct me; and I hope gentlemen will become convinced during the discussion, that the case which so many of them have stated, of any foreign power succoring and protecting the revolted slaves of the southern states, is not the parallel of that before us. As to the first point, it is to be recollected, that some years past, to quote from high authority, "during the agonizing spasms of infuriated man, seeking through blood and slaughter his long lost liberties," when our enlightened sister Republic of France was, in her abundant kindness, forcing liberty upon all the world, and propagating the rights of man at the point of the bayonet, in one of her paroxysms of philanthropy, she proclaimed, by a solemn decree of her Convention, the blessings of liberty and equality to the blacks of Santo Domingo too; invited them to the fraternal embrace, and to the honors of a Conventional sitting.

The wisdom or the policy of this proceeding, it is not my business to inquire into, but it certainly affords some excuse, if any be necessary, for the subsequent conduct of those unfortunate people. The decree abolishing forever slavery in the West Indies, (French,) and extending all the blessings of citizenship and equality to every human creature, of whatever grade or color, then under the Government of France, passed the Convention in February, 1794. The existence of such a paper I did not expect would have been doubted here till the gentleman from New Jersey (Mr. Kitchel) actually denied it . . .

And this same principle the Convention frequently recognized, by receiving at their bar, in the most complimentary manner, various deputations of blacks from the West Indies, thanking them for the boon conferred upon them. One of these instances, among many others, I will submit, as a curiosity in legislative proceedings, to the Senate: "National Convention. Order of the day. A band of blacks of both sexes, amidst the sound of martial music, and escorted by a great band of Parisians, came into the hall to return thanks to the Legislature for having raised them to the rank of men. The President gave the fraternal kiss to an old Negress, 114 years old, and mother of eleven children. After which she was respectfully conducted to an armed chair and seated by the side of the President, amid the loudest bursts of applause . . ."

We have here their liberty solemnly recognized and proclaimed to the world eight years afterwards by the man who was then and still is at the head of the French Government; or rather, who is now the Government itself. I cite these papers to show that the French have now no claim, either in right, in justice, or in law, to any portion of the people of Santo Domingo as slaves; that they are individually free, if the highest authorities in France could constitute them so, which will surely not be questioned; and in order to rebut a fallacious idea that has been taken up, and urged by some, that our merchants are conducting this commerce with slaves, the property of freemen, and not with freemen themselves, thus ingeniously endeavoring to draw a distinction between the situation of Santo Domingo and that of any other colony that has ever heretofore attempted to separate itself from the mother country; to make theirs, according to the language of the gentleman from Virginia, (Mr. Moore,) a totally new, unprecedented case, and in this manner to take them out of the humane provisions of the laws of nations. I grant, sir, their case does form a distinction from any other, and in this it consists: the people of Santo Domingo are fighting to preserve not only their independence as a community, but their liberty as individuals; to prevent a degradation from the exalted state of freemen to the debased condition of slaves, struggling against the manacles that have been forged for them by the lawless ambition of power. . . .

I must here inquire if, as gentlemen contend, it is not now lawful to carry on commerce with the people of Santo Domingo, when it may probably become so? Suppose, for instance, the French should continue this inefficient kind of warfare upon them, if even such it may be considered, for a century to come, holding as at present but a single post in the island, while the natives are in full possession of the sovereignty of the country, and administering a regular government? Will it be said, under such circumstances, that no nation is to be allowed to trade with them for a century to come? Or will gentlemen hold them as rebels to all eternity, and never suffer the rest of the world to have intercourse with them? Sir, those people will never be reduced by General Ferrand's war of proclamations; and while on this subject I must be permitted to express my astonishment at a very extraordinary document of this kind that has been recently laid upon our tables, signed by General Ferrand, and purporting to be a proclamation or decree of his, directed chiefly at the citizens and commerce of the United States. It is indeed, throughout, calculated to inspire no other sentiment than contempt; the arrogance and presumption of its style and manner is equaled only by the emptiness of its threats.

General Ferrand, shut up in the city of Santo Domingo, with scarcely the power of conveying his proclamation beyond the redoubts of his garrison, undertakes to prescribe to all the neutral nations of the earth the extent of their rights, and the manner in which they shall conduct their commerce, and expresses truly great surprise that his former decree on the subject had not been better attended to by them; in which, as he says, he had "left no doubt as to the sentiments of respect due to the freedom of navigation and neutral rights." As if the navigation, the commerce, and all the rights of neutral nations depended now upon the caprice of a French officer, and were, like the police of a camp, to be settled by general orders. And this same Captain General, as he calls himself, *pro tempore,* besieged by a parcel of unarmed, undisciplined, half-starved Negroes, without the means of making even a sortie upon them, talks of the *impudence* of our public officers, and threatens with the vengeance of his mighty arm, all the people of the United States that go contrary to his orders.

Sir, I can liken this proclamation to nothing but the idle vaporings of a fettered maniac, menacing from the grates of his cell, the overthrow of the world. If the Pope had issued a bull of excommunication against the whole of us, it could not have been half so ridiculous as this proclamation, upon which the gentleman from Maryland on my left (Mr. Wright) has inadvertently rested as one of the strongholds of his argument; telling us, to use his own words, that it was a requisition too imperious to be resisted. Then, sir, such is the ground we now occupy among nations, that the mandate of a French officer, besieged in the West Indies by a rabble of starving Negroes, is a requisition too imperious for us to resist. Were I of opinion with that honorable member, I should at once be for soliciting the protection of those blacks, and praying of them, in Heaven's name, to keep where he is this mighty warrior, this terror of our land . . .

5. Thomas Moore Denounces Jeffersonian America, 1806.

Tom Moore was an Irish poet who preferred English patronage to revolutionary politics. After trying a minor civil service job in Bermuda, he toured the United States in 1804, enjoying the hospitality of Anthony Merry and a number of arch-Federalists. His views of American politics were formed by such company, as is clear from the verses below. His railing against the United States unfortunately found a responsive audience in England. Years later, his fame and income now being secured by a series of immensely popular "Irish Songs," he published an apology to the people of the United States. [Originally published in *Epistles, Odes and Other Poems*, 1806; text from *The Poetical Works of Thomas Moore* (London, 1908), pp. 143–144.]

From Epistle VI. To Lord Viscount Forbes, from the City of Washington.

Already in this free, this virtuous state,
Which, Frenchmen tell us, was ordained by Fate,
To show the world what high perfection springs
From rabble senators and merchant kings—
Even here already patriots learn to steal
Their private perquisite from public weal,
And, guardians of the country's sacred fire,
Like Afric's priests, they let the flame for hire!
Those vaunted demagogues, who nobly rose
From England's debtors to be England's foes,
Who could their monarch in their purse forget,
And break allegiance but to cancel debt,
Have proved at length the mineral's tempting hue
Which makes a patriot, can unmake him too.

❋　　❋　　❋

Who can, with patience, for a moment see
The medley mass of pride and misery,
Of whips and charters, manacles and rights,
Of slaving blacks and democratic whites,
And all the piebald polity that reigns
In free confusion o'er Columbia's plains?
To think that man, thou just and gentle God
Should stand before thee, with a tyrant's rod
O'er creatures like himself, with soul from thee,
Yet dare to boast of perfect liberty:
Away, away—I'd rather hold my neck
By doubtful tenure from a sultan's beck,
In climes where liberty has scarce been named,
Nor any right but that of ruling claimed,
Than thus to live, where bastard freedom waves
Her fustian flag in mockery over slaves;
Where (motley laws admitting no degree
Betwixt the vilely slaved and madly free)
Alike the bondage and the license suit,
The brute made ruler and the man made brute!

6. Fisher Ames on Napoleon, March, 1806.

In the early months of 1806, the Congress of the United States debated the wisdom of an embargo against all trade with the British Empire, the theory being the familiar one that British attacks on our shipping must yield to the inescapable dependence of Britain upon our markets and our raw materials. As these debates wore on, Napoleon was rapidly bringing continental Europe under his power. Ames, who had retired from the House of Representatives in 1797, was not likely to make many converts to his notion that the United States should subordinate itself to Britain's fight against Napoleon, especially since he described the Americans who needed convincing as being an ignorant rabble! Ames died in 1808, and his funeral was a sort of Federalist rally against the Embargo, which finally had been established. [Seth Ames, ed., *Works of Fisher Ames* (Boston, 1854), II, 285–87.]

The Successes of Bonaparte

The rapid and decisive successes of Bonaparte have inflated the ignorant rabble of our democrats with admiration, and filled every reflecting mind with astonishment and terror. The means that most men deemed adequate to the reduction of his power have failed of their effect, and have gone to swell the colossal mass that oppresses Europe; his foes are become his satellites. Austria, the German states, Prussia, Naples, and perhaps Sweden, seem to have been fated, like comets, to a shock with the sun, not to thrust him from his orb, but to supply his waste of elemental fire. Bonaparte not only sees the prowess of Europe at his feet, but all its force and treasure in his hands. We except Russia and England. But Russia is one of those comets on its excursion into the void regions of space, and is already dim in the political sky; England passes, like Mercury, a dark spot over the sun's disk; and to Bonaparte himself she seems, like the moon, to intercept his rays. He cannot endure to see her so near his splendor, without being dazzled or consumed by it. He wants nothing but the British navy to realize the most extravagant schemes of his ambition. A war that should humble England, and withdraw her navy from any further opposition to his arms, would give the civilized world a master. All the French, and of course all our loyal democrats, have affected to treat that apprehension as chimerical. Yet who, even among those whom faction has made most blind, could refuse to see that the transfer of the British navy to France would irreversibly fix the long-depending destiny of mankind, to bear the weight and ignominy of a new Roman domination.

We may say the aggravated weight, for Rome preserved her morals till she had achieved her conquests; France begins her career as deeply corrupt as Rome ended it. The Roman republic, after having grown to a gigantic stature from its soundness, rotted when it died; but that of France, surviving the principles, and at length the name of a republic, has drawn aliment from disease, and we of this generation have seen it crawl, like some portentous serpent from a tomb, glistening and bloated with venom from its loathsome banquet. France has owed the progress of her arms to the prevalence of her vices. These were the causes of the revolution; and the revolution has in turn made these the instruments of French aggrandizement. By the persecution of all that was virtue, the leaders gave encouragement to all that was vice; and thus they not only acquired the power to spend the nation's last shilling, but imparted to the rabble all the ardor of enthusiasm, and all the energies that the love of novelty, of plunder, and of vengeance could inspire. The means they commanded were not such as arise from the just and orderly government of a state, but from its dissolution. The priests, the rich, and the nobles, were offered as human sacrifices on the altar of the revolution, and still more emphatically of French ambition.

Thus France, like Polyphème in his cave, grew fat with carnage. Other states could not, without submitting to a like revolution, oppose her with equal arms. So far from it, they found that all those whom vice and want had made the enemies of the laws of their country, were banded together as the friends of France.

Thus it was that the French armies no sooner entered Italy than they arrayed in arms an Italian rabble, to hold all those who had anything to lose, in fear and inactivity, till they could be regularly plundered. The leaders of this rabble were invested with the mock dignities of the Cisalpine government. The like was done in Holland and Switzerland.

The new yoke, therefore, which the abject nations are so near taking on their necks, cannot be light. That France may rule everywhere, the worst of men must be permitted everywhere to rule in the worst of ways. The Roman yoke was iron, and it crushed as well as wearied the provinces; but the domination of culprits and outlaws, claiming much for themselves, and exacting more for their masters in France, will place the people between the upper and the nether millstone.

If the miserable dupes of France, so loyal to the commands of her envoy, can wish destruction to the British navy, and can really think American liberty the safer for its future tenure by the good pleasure of Bonaparte, such men are certainly fitter subjects for medicine than argument; where such sentiments do not spring from the rottenness of the heart, they must escape through some crack in the brain.

There was a time when the infatuation in favor of France was a popular malady. If that time has so far passed over that men can either think or feel as Americans ought, it must be apparent that Bonaparte wants but little, and is enraged that he so long wants that little, to be the world's master. Yet at this awful crisis, when the British navy alone prevents his final success, we of the United States come forward, with an ostentation of hostility to England, to annoy her with nonintercourse laws. Are we determined to leave nothing to chance, but to volunteer our industry in forging our chains?

7. Madison's Instructions to Monroe and Pinkney, 17 May 1806.

While Fisher Ames frightened the citizens of Massachusetts with the prospect of future revolutions and invasions, Thomas

Jefferson and James Madison still were contriving ways to turn the European war to America's advantage. They expected the new British ministry under Charles James Fox to be much friendlier to the United States than its predecessors. Believing also that the commercial restrictions sanctioned by Congress would force Britain to concede our moderate demands, the President and the Secretary of State confidently awaited the restoration of good Anglo-American relations. The instructions have been heavily edited here for want of space, but perhaps enough appears to demonstrate how complex, elaborate, and confusing the diplomacy of neutral rights was becoming. James Monroe was then our minister to England, and William Pinkney of Maryland joined him as special envoy with new instructions. [Gaillard Hunt, ed., *The Writings of James Madison* (New York, 1908), VII, 375–86, 391–93.]

. . . It is [the President's] particular wish that the British Government should be made fully to understand that the United States are sincerely and anxiously disposed to cherish good will and liberal intercourse between the two nations, that an unwillingness alone to take measures not congenial with that disposition has made them so long patient under violations of their rights and of the rules of a friendly reciprocity; and when forced at length by accumulating wrongs to depart from an absolute forbearance, they have not only selected a mode strictly pacific, but in demonstration of their friendly policy, have connected with the measure, an extraordinary mission, with powers to remove every source of difference, and even to enlarge the foundations of future harmony and mutual interest.

There can be the less ground of umbrage to the British Government, in the Act prohibiting the importation of certain articles of British manufacture, 1st because there is nothing on the face of the Act beyond a mere commercial regulation, tending to foster manufactures in the United States, to lessen our dependence on a single nation by the distribution of our trade, and to substitute for woolens and linens, manufactures made from one of our principal agricultural staples. 2nd because it is far short of a reciprocity with British exclusions of American articles of export. 3d because as a commercial measure discriminating in time of war, between British and other nations, it has examples in British practice. It deserves attention also that a discrimination was made, and under another name still exists, in the amount of convoy duty imposed on the trade between Great Britain with Europe, and with America. 4th because the measure cannot be ascribed to a partiality towards the enemies of Great Britain, or to a view of favoring them in the war; having for its sole object the interest of the United States, which it pursues in a mode strictly conformable to the rights and the practice of all nations.

. . . The first article of the project comprised in the instructions of 1804, relates to the impressment of seamen. The importance of an effectual remedy for this practice, derives urgency from the licentiousness with which it is still pursued, and from the growing impatience of this country under it. So indispensable is some adequate provision for the case, that the President makes it a necessary preliminary to any stipulation requiring a repeal of the Act shutting the market of the United States against certain British manufactures. At the same time he authorizes you in case the ultimatum as stated in the Article above referred to, should not be acceptable to the British Government, to substitute one in the terms of the following —"No seaman nor seafaring person shall upon the high seas, and without the jurisdiction of either party, be demanded or taken out of any ship or vessel, belonging to the citizens or subjects of one of the parties, by the public or private armed ships or men of war belonging to or in the service of the other party; and strict orders shall be given for the observance of this engagement." . . .

With respect to contraband which is the subject of the 4th article, it may be observed that as it excludes naval stores from the list, and is otherwise limited to articles strictly military, it must be admissible to Great Britain, [and] leave but feeble objections to an abolition of contraband altogether. In the present state of the arts in Europe, with the intercourse by land, no nation at war with Great Britain can be much embarrassed by leaving those particular articles subject to maritime capture. Whilst belligerent nations therefore have little interest in the limited right against contraband, it imposes on neutrals all the evils resulting from suspicious and vexatious searches, and from questions incident to the terms used in the actual enumeration. It is not an unreasonable hope therefore, that in place of this article, an entire abolition of contraband may be substituted. Should this be found unattainable, it may be an improvement of the Article, as it stands, to subjoin for the sake of greater caution to the positive enumeration, a negative specification of certain articles, such as provisions, money, naval stores, etc. as in no case to be deemed within the meaning of the article with a proviso, that the specification shall not be construed to imply in the least, that any articles not specified in the exception, shall on that account be liable to be drawn into question.

A doctrine has been lately introduced by the British Courts and at length adopted by the instructions of June 1803, to British cruisers, which regards contraband conveyed in one voyage as affecting a resumed or returning voyage, although contraband shall have been previously deposited at its port of destination. It will be a further improvement of the Article to insert a declaratory clause against the innovation, and the abuses incident to it.

The 4th Article, besides the stipulation on the subject of contraband, relates to two other subjects; 1st that of free ships free goods, 2nd that of a trade with enemy's colonies.

1st. With respect to the first, the principle that a neutral flag covers the property of an enemy, is relinquished, in pursuance of the example of the Russian Treaty on which the article is modeled; the relinquishment however being connected with and conditioned on, the provision required in favor of the neutral right to the colonial trade. The importance of that principle to the security of neutral commerce, and to the freedom of the seas, has at all times been felt by the United States; and although they have not asserted it as the established law of nations, they have ever been anxious to see it made a part of that law. It was with reluctance, of course, that a contrary stipulation was authorized, and merely as a mean of obtaining from Great Britain, the recognition of a principle now become of more importance to neutral nations possessing mercantile capital, than the principle of "free ships free goods." It is to be particularly kept in view therefore that such a contrary stipulation is to be avoided if possible, and if unavoidable that the stipulation be so modified as to interfere as little as possible with the spirit and policy of any provisions in favor of the principle which may be likely to be introduced into a treaty of peace among the present belligerent powers of Europe. Should it be known that Russia as well as France meant to insist on such a provision, and that such a stipulation by the United States however modified, will naturally affect her confidence and good will towards them, the objection to the measure will acquire a force that can yield only to the consideration that without such a sacrifice the provisions for the security of our seamen, and our neutral commerce, cannot be obtained and that the sacrifice will effectually answer these purposes.

2d. The vast importance of the colonial trade, with the circumstances and the excitement which have taken place since the date of the original instructions to Mr. Monroe, will require that the neutral right on this subject, be provided for in an appropriate article, and in terms more explicit than are used in the article under review. As the right in this case, turns on the general principle that neutrals may lawfully trade, with the exception of blockades and contraband, to and between all ports of an enemy and in all articles, although the trade shall not have been open to them in time of peace, particular care is to be taken that no part of the principle be expressly or virtually abandoned, as being no part of the law of nations. On the contrary it is much to be desired that the general principle in its full extent, be laid down in the stipulation. But as this may not be attainable and as too much ought not to be risked by an inflexible pursuit of abstract right, especially against the example and the sentiments of great powers having concurrent interests with the United States; you are left at liberty if found necessary to abridge the right in practice, as it is done in the supplement of October 1801 to the Treaty of June of that year, between Russia and Great Britain; not omitting to provide that in case Great Britain should by her Treaties or instructions leave to any other nation the right in a greater extent than it is stipulated to the United States, they may claim the enjoyment of it in an equal extent.

The abuses which have been committed by Great Britain under the pretext that a neutral trade, from enemy colonies, through neutral ports, was a direct trade, render it indispensable to guard against such a pretext by some express declaration on that point. The most that can be conceded on the part of the United States, is that the landing of the goods, the securing the duties, and the change of the ship, or preferably the landing of the goods alone, or with the securing the duties, shall be requisite to destroy the identity of the voyage and the directness of the trade, and that the ordinary documents of the Custom House officers, shall be sufficient evidence of the facts or fact.

A satisfactory provision on this subject of a trade with enemy colonies, is deemed of so much consequence to the rights and interests of the United States, and is so well understood to have been contemplated along with a like provision against the impressment of seamen, in the late Act of Congress prohibiting the importation of certain classes of British manufactures that, as was enjoined with respect to the provision against impressment, no stipulation is to be entered into not consistent with a continuance of that Act, unless the provision with respect to the colonial trade is also obtained. . . .

In addition to what is proposed on the subject of blockades in VI and VII articles, the perseverance of Great Britain in considering a notification of a blockade, and even of an intended blockade, to a foreign government, or its ministers at London, as a notice to its citizens, and as rendering a vessel wherever found in a destination to the notified port, as liable to capture, calls for a special remedy. The palpable injustice of the practice, is aggravated by the auxiliary rule prevailing in the British Courts, that the blockade is to be held in legal force, until the governmental notification be expressly rescinded; however certain the fact may be that the blockade was never formed or had ceased. You will be at no loss for topics to enforce the inconsistency of these innovations upon the law of nations, with the nature of blockades, with the safety of neutral commerce; and particularly with the communication made to this Government by order of the British Government in the year 1804; according to which the British commanders and Vice Admiralty Courts, were instructed "not to consider any blockade of the islands of Martinique and Guadeloupe as existing unless in respect of particular ports which may be actually invested, and then not to capture vessels bound to such ports unless they shall previously have been warned not to enter them."

The absurdity of substituting such diplomatic notifications in place of a special warning from the blockading ships cannot be better illustrated than by the fact, that before the notification of a proposed blockade of Cadiz in the year 1805 was received here from our minister at London, official information was received form Cadiz, that the blockade had actually been raised, by an enemy's fleet.

❈   ❈   ❈

There remains as an object of great importance, some adequate provision against the insults and injuries committed by British cruisers in the vicinity of our shores and harbors. These have been heretofore a topic of remonstrance, and have in a late instance, been repeated with circumstances peculiarly provoking, as they include the murder of an American seaman within the jurisdictional limits the United States. Mr. Monroe is in full possession of the documents explaining a former instance. Herewith will be received those relating to the late one. They not only support a just demand of an exemplary punishment of the offenders and of indemnity for the spoliations, but call for some stipulations guarding against such outrages in future. With this view it is proper that all armed belligerent ships should be expressly and effectually restrained from making seizures or searches within a certain distance from our coast, or taking stations near our harbors, commodious for those purposes. . . .

Another object not comprehended in the instructions of 1804 to Mr. Monroe, is rendered important by the number of illegal captures and injuries, which have been committed by British cruisers since that date. An indemnity for them is due on every consideration of justice and friendship and is enforced by the example heretofore given by Great Britain herself, as well as by other nations which have provided by treaty for repairing the spoliations practised under color of their authority. You will press this as an object too reasonable not to be confidently expected by the United States. Many of the claims indeed for indemnification are so obviously just that a refusal to satisfy them, cannot be decently made, and ought not therefore to be presumed. . . .

But as relates to the West Indies and North American colonies it must be a permanent object of the United States, to have the intercourse with them made as free as that with Europe. The relative situation of the United States and those colonies, and particularly those wants which we can alone supply, must necessarily produce that effect at some no very distant period. And it should not be voluntarily retarded either by abandoning by treaty the strong hold which our right of stopping the intercourse gives us; or by accepting any temporary or trifling privilege, the exercise of which would diminish the probability of soon obtaining a perfectly free trade. . . .

The minimum which should be accepted in relation to the intercourse with the West Indies, will be the admission of our vessels laden solely with articles of our growth, produce, or manufacture, the importation of which [in] British vessels is not prohibited, on the same terms as British vessels solely laden with the colonial articles shall be admitted in our ports, that is to say, either without alien duties or with a fixed maximum of such alien duties with the two following restrictions. 1st. That Great Britain may prohibit our vessels from exporting from the British West India Islands in sugar and coffee, more than one half of the proceeds of their inward cargoes. 2dly. That such sugar and coffee shall be exported only to the United States, or that the vessels thus admitted in the West Indies shall be obliged to return and land their cargoes in the United States, provided they may however, on their return touch at any other West India Island or the Bahamas to complete their cargo. For it is usual to carry the specie which proceeds from the sale of a cargo in the West Indies to Turks Island or the Bahamas and there load with salt for the United States. Although those restrictions and particularly the first be inconvenient, yet they may be acquiesced in. . . .

8. Albert Gallatin Expects War after the Chesapeake-Leopard Outrage, 17 July 1807.

The negotiation of Monroe and Pinkney seemed so promising in the fall of 1806 that the United States suspended its restrictions on British trade. But for all their impeccable Democratic-Republicanism, the two ministers signed a treaty quite like that of John Jay's of 1794. There was no article on impressment, no invitation for American ships to visit the British West Indies, and no provision such as Jay had secured to recover damages for ships unfairly captured and condemned. Monroe and Pinkney could say, as Jay had said, that the treaty still offered great commercial opportunities to the United States and perhaps a basis for more concessions later. Jefferson and Madison rejected the treaty without sending it to the Senate, but they also left the restrictions on British trade suspended and urged their ministers to continue negotiations in a friendly manner. Napoleon's continuing success in bringing Europe under his command should, in Jefferson's view, have made the British more compliant. But it had the opposite effect, and Napoleon's Berlin Decree of 21 November 1806 produced in 1807 a series of British counterdecrees that made neutrality impossible. As this unpleasant situation progressed, the most startling instance of impressment in our history took place. *H.M.S. Leopard* fired on the defenseless frigate *Chesapeake*, boarded her, and removed four deserters from the British Navy. American sailors died in the engagement, so that to the insult to our flag was added the outrage of murder.

Albert Gallatin, Secretary of the Treasury, was the last man to invoke war as an instrument of national policy. To him, progress meant steady commercial and industrial growth, and he dreaded as much as Hamilton ever had the effect upon his precious public revenue of a war with Britain. But he saw war as a nearly inevitable result of the *Chesapeake-Leopard affair*. [Letter to Joseph H. Nicholson. Henry Adams, ed., *The Writings of Albert Gallatin* (Philadelphia, 1879), I, 338–40.]

. . . With you, I believe that war is inevitable; and there can be but one opinion on the question whether the claims of the parties prior to the attack on the *Chesapeake* should be a subject of discussion. There were but two courses to be taken,—either to consider the attack as war, and retaliate immediately, or, on the supposition that that act might be that of an unauthorized officer, to ask simply, and without discussion, disavowal, satisfaction, and security against a recurrence of outrages. The result will, in my opinion, be the same, for Great Britain will not, I am confident, give either satisfaction or security; but the latter mode, which, as you may have perceived by the President's proclamation and his answer to military corps, has been adopted, was recommended not only by the nature of our Constitution, which does not make the President arbiter of war, but also by the practice of civilized nations; and the cases of Turk's Island, Falkland Islands, Nootka Sound, etc., are in point in that respect. Add to this that the dissatisfaction caused by that course operates only against the Administration, and that the other will produce an unanimity in support of the war which would not otherwise have existed. It will also make our cause completely popular with the Baltic powers, and may create new enemies to Britain in that quarter. Finally, four months were of importance to us, both by diminishing the losses of our merchants and for preparations of defense and attack.

I will, however, acknowledge that on that particular point I have not bestowed much thought, for, having considered from the first moment war as a necessary result, and the preliminaries appearing to me but matters of form, my faculties have been exclusively applied to the preparations necessary to meet the times; and although I am not very sanguine as to the brilliancy of our exploits, the field where we can act without a navy being very limited, and perfectly aware that a war in a great degree passive and consisting of privations will become very irksome to the people, I feel no apprehension of the ultimate result. We will be poorer, both as a nation and as a government, our debt and taxes will increase, and our progress in every respect be interrupted. But all those evils are not only not to be put in competition with the independence and honor of the nation; they are, moreover, temporary, and very few years of peace will obliterate their effects. Nor do I know whether the awakening of nobler feelings and habits than avarice and luxury might not be necessary to prevent our degenerating, like the Hollanders, into a nation of mere calculators. In fact, the greatest mischiefs which I apprehend from the war are the necessary increase of executive power and influence, the speculations of contractors and jobbers, and the introduction of permanent military and naval establishments.

Money we will want to carry on the war; our revenue will be cut up; new and internal taxes will be slow and not sufficiently productive; we must necessarily borrow. This is not pleasing particularly to me; but it must be done; for whilst we must avoid expenses for inefficient operations and waste, as far as is practicable, the expense, provided we can by any method whatever defray it, must never be an objection to any necessary measure of defense, or to any rational active operations against the enemy. We have about eight millions in the Treasury, and from a very rough estimate I think that we will want to borrow about ten millions annually while the war lasts; rather less, however, the first year, although it will be the most expensive. People will fight, but they never give their money for nothing. Patriotic gifts and loyalty loans cannot be depended upon; we must buy money at its market price, and in order to borrow cheaper it will be necessary to keep up the price of stocks by occasional purchases. All this is, of course, between ourselves. But as I think that our first loans must be obtained from the banks, and you are a bank director, I will thank you to sound the ground on that subject. With the Bank of the United States I will treat separately; but the best course would perhaps [be] that the directors of all the other banks of Baltimore should consult together and see what in their opinion might be loaned. From the extent of banking capital there and the great diminution which will take place in commerce, and therefore in their business, I am confident they might lend one half of their capital to government without any inconvenience either to the mercantile interest or to themselves. The periods both of their advance and of the reimbursement, as well as the manner of throwing the thing into form, would be a matter of detail. Will you consult with General Smith, who is connected with other banks, on that subject? I will write to him about it today or tomorrow. I mean to make similar informal overtures in the other seaports; and it would have a good effect both here and abroad to be able to state to Congress that resources are already prepared. The war may be of shorter continuance if the enemy receives an early impression that we are willing and able to hold out.

9. John Love of Virginia Defends the Embargo, 18 April 1808.

Jefferson and Madison tried to use the *Chesapeake-Leopard* outrage as the basis for a sweeping settlement with Britain, supposing that the unmistakable willingness of Americans to declare war and the undeniable aggression of the *Leopard*

would force compliance with our terms. But the intense and
expanding commercial warfare between France and Britain
shattered whatever rights neutrals had preserved. When
Britain refused our proposals, the United States resorted to
Madison's favorite device of commercial restrictions. The Embargo of December, 1807, absolutely halted imports to and
exports from the United States and therefore stood as a protest
against French as well as British claims to license and control
world trade. A minority in Congress tried to repeal or sus-
pend the Embargo in April, 1808, but it survived for almost
a year and then was replaced with more selective forms of
commercial restriction. Representative John Love was an able
supporter of the policies of Jefferson and Madison; his defense of the Embargo met especially the attacks of the maverick Virginian John Randolph. [Thomas Hart Benton, ed.,
Abridgement of the Debates of Congress (New York, 1857),
III, 679–81.]

. . . That the embargo was a curse, and continues to be a most
calamitous one to us all, I have heard no one deny; but until now,
I have not heard the assertion advanced that our Government, by
its conduct, was the author of that curse. Yes, sir, many evils which
the injustice of other nations has inflicted on the peace and honor
of the United States are acknowledged to be curses of the most ir-
ritating and affecting nature; but the gentleman has said more for
England and France, than either of them has before said for itself,
when he attributes to his own Government the misconduct which has
produced those evils. It was scarcely to be expected that any state
of internal division or any views of whatever description would have
produced on this floor an assertion which has thus put a new argument in the hands of our enemies in justification of their aggressions
on us; it is more than our enemies have asserted. We have heard
indeed from France and England that their decrees and orders,
which make the present voluntary retirement from the seas necessary
on our part, were the effect of an unjustifiable attack, which each
has attributed in the first instance to the other. Each criminates the
other, and not America, with being the author of the peculiar mode
of warfare which has proved so destructive to the rights of neutrals.
The very language of their orders and decrees assumes this position,

and they are all prefaced with the declaration, that their orders are enacted in the spirit of retaliation on each other, and not, sir, for any offense which our Government has been the author of, as the gentleman now tells the American people; for what purpose let the nation judge. . . .

The opinions then avowed, sir, by the advocates of the embargo, have met with support from the events which have since developed, while the unjustifiable grounds of opposition are abandoned, even by their authors. But, sir, if there is any gentleman, who, with his eyes open to the situation of the commerce of the world, will say that the embargo ought to be removed, and that the policy is unsound, let me ask him to tell us what, in the embarrassing state in which we are placed by the efforts of France and England to involve us in their conflicts, we are to do? The gentleman from Virginia has hinted at arming our merchantmen! War, then, is the substitute; it is, indeed, the only one, I agree. To arm our merchantmen, leads to war—nay, sir, it is war, according to the interpretation nations have a right to put on such an act of a Government; it will be opposed by open war and undisguised hostility. If we are to have war, let it be in the direct tone and unequivocal language of a nation indignant at the insults it has received, not in the indirect manner of arming a few trading vessels, the masters of whom would choose for the nation its enemy, or involve us with both the belligerents at once, as their particular animosities might dictate; if we are to go to war, it might be well to fight one at a time at least.

But, sir, I cannot but hope if our strong, but pacific policy is adhered to, cursed as it is said to be, it may yet preserve us from the conflicts of Europe. It is a curse, indeed, sir, under which we are compelled to labor, but what is the alternative? I have thought much, sir, on the subject; it has been my duty as well as that of every other gentleman to weigh it well. We hear its effects are severely felt, and we hear, too, what are the exertions of our opponents to seize the favorite opportunity which it is so well calculated to produce, to excite the sensibility of the people through the medium of their immediate interests. But remove the embargo, and we must arm our vessels, and war is at once declared. I have heard no one deny that this must be the alternative. Compare the evils, both of great extent. I admit, by the embargo, we lose half the value of the products of our country, or the receipt of it is suspended; by war, to admit the effect in this particular, no worse, at least it could be no better; but have we counted the costs of the armies we are to raise, and to pay, of the supplies we are to furnish, of the loss of our blood, and the diminution of our strength, of the reduction of the profits of agriculture itself, by calling men from their domestic occupations, and lessening the number of hands for tillage—have we calculated the thousand other evils which follow in the train of war?

To plunge into war, sir, to escape the curse of the embargo, would be truly fulfilling the adage of old—"out of the frying-pan into the fire." I do not hesitate to say that, if we have patriotism enough to pursue our own interests, better would it be for this country to remain under the truly calamitous curse of the embargo for years, than at once to launch itself into war. But if we must at length, after all our efforts to prevent it, have war, let it be a war dependent on national sentiment, and arising from no doubtful necessity, which must be produced by the conflicts of our vessels at sea. . . .

10. John Randolph Mentions Some Disadvantages of the Embargo, 19 April 1808.

John Randolph's motives could well be doubted, so often did he oppose the measures of his government. But for all his perversity, he had a talent for finding the weakness or the danger contained within a policy or a course of action. The following speech reveals the demoralizing and divisive effects of commercial restriction. [Benton, *Abridgement of the Debates of Congress*, III, 706–7.]

. . . Why, when the embargo was laid, there were those who made money on it, because they got earlier intelligence of it than their fellow citizens; and now, when the embargo is in operation, there are those who do not suffer under it. I have it from good information, that at least 100,000 barrels of flour have been shipped from Balti-

more alone since it was laid. It may be recollected, that the gentleman from Maryland, who, the other day, gave us so able an illus-
tration of the question, urged as an argument against it, that the
embargo operated unequally. I should be sorry to put myself on a
par with that gentleman in any knowledge, much less could I assume
to possess a better knowledge of his own district than he himself
possesses; but I believe it has been said by a gentleman said to be
possessed of commercial knowledge, that many thousand barrels of
flour had been shipped from that gentleman's district alone through
Baltimore. I was in hopes that this reply would have been made
before, because, coming from the quarter whence it must have come,
it would have operated as an argument to estimate the value of this
measure on the West India Islands; and it is evident, that nothing
but an evasion of this kind would keep up the price, low as it is—
for, when I single out Baltimore, I have no doubt the same game
is going on elsewhere—at Eastern Point and Passamaquoddy particularly. The operation of the embargo is to furnish rogues with
an opportunity of getting rich at the expense of honest men. The
man who is hardy enough to give bond and leave his security in
the lurch, can make great returns; whereas the honest merchant and
planter are suffering at home, and bearing the burden. It is for the
benefit of the dishonest trader—for the planter is out of the question,
as he cannot be a partner in the act which contravenes the law of
the land.

Is this all the operation of the embargo? No; for I will tell you
another operation it has; that while the sheriff is hunting the citizen
from bailiwick to bailiwick with a writ, his produce lying on his
hands worth nothing, your shaving gentry—accommodation men,
five per cent per month men—are making fifty or sixty per cent by
usury; or making still more by usury of a worse sort—buying the
property of their neighbor at less than one half its value: and well
they may afford to appropriate their money to such profitable uses,
supposing character, morals, religion, honor, and every thing dear
to man, trodden under foot by Mammon. Are these alone the effects
which result from the embargo? No, sir; you are teaching your
merchants, on whose fidelity, on whose sacred observation of an
oath, when the course of events returns to its natural channel, your

whole revenue depends; you are putting them to school, and must expect to take the consequences of their education. You are, by the pressure of the embargo, which is almost too strong for human nature, laying calculations and snares in the way, teaching them to disregard their oath for the sake of profit; and do you expect your commerce to return to its natural channel without smuggling? You may take all your Navy, and gunboats into the bargain, with all which you cannot stop them. Those men who now export so many barrels of flour from our markets, will not pay the high duties on wines and groceries when they can avoid it by evasion of the laws; for they will have learned the art of evading laws; they will have taken their degrees in the school of the embargo. This is the necessary result. You lay temptations before them too strong for their virtue to resist, and then, having cast your daughters into a brothel, you expect them to come out pure and uncontaminated. It is out of the question, and I venture to predict that the effect of this measure upon our imposts and our morals too, sir, will be felt when not one man in this assembly shall be alive. Every arrival from the West Indies tells you of the cargoes of flour daily carried in, until it becomes a point of honor not to tell one another.

11. An Anti-Embargo Catechism, 1808.

Why is the Embargo like sickness?
Because it weakens us.

Why is it like a whirlwind?
Because we can't tell certainly where it came from or where it is going;
   it knocks some down, breaks others, and turns everything topsy-turvy.

Why is it like hydrophobia?
Because it makes us dread the water.
If you spell it backward what does it say?
O grab me!

[Quoted from an unnamed newspaper by John Bach McMaster, *History of the People of the United States III;* New York, 1891; 291.]

12. Rufus King Has Little Hope, 9 April 1809.

Although the Embargo certainly hurt British manufacturers and West Indies planters, it was abandoned in February, 1809, because of domestic opposition. The Federalists regained control of New England in the 1808 elections, and the state courts were balking at the laws required to enforce the Embargo with the rigor required for success. A new non-intercourse law prohibited trade with Britain and France but authorized the executive to resume trade with either power that recognized American rights.

The Non-Intercourse Act was weak, because under its terms, American ships could sail beyond the reach of American law merely by declaring an intention to trade with some nation other than France or Britain. Early in 1809, it appeared that both the United States and British leaders were so eager for a settlement that they were prepared to make significant concessions. Merry's successor, David Montagu Erskine, genuinely wished for reconciliation. His personal contribution was impressive: he married the daughter of General John Cadwalader, an American Revolutionary hero, and produced twelve Anglo-American children. Erskine departed from his instructions to form a treaty in April, 1809, whereupon the United States reopened commerce with Britain while continuing to prohibit it with France. These events were just unfolding when Rufus King wrote the following letter to Christopher Gore of Massachusetts. King was especially excited by the sequel to Napoleon's attempt to force his brother upon the Spanish people. The Spanish revolt of 1808 had weakened Napoleon and practically cut off Spanish America from European control. [Charles R. King, ed., *The Life and Correspondence of Rufus King* (New York, 1898), V, 151–52.]

. . . The campaign in Spain has thus far proceeded as I have constantly believed it would do, except that the English army has been withdrawn without as great losses as I apprehended it would sustain. Perhaps a portion of this army may be re-embarked for Cadiz and Gibraltar, but the peninsula must be conquered by Bonaparte. Our best hope is that the chiefs with a portion of the people will escape and proceed to South America. Thus the failure in Europe will hasten the epoch of the independence of the Spanish colonies. How blind must our rulers have been to have remained until this day, unconvinced of, and unprepared for, this great event. The success of Bonaparte in Spain is matter of regret here, and everywhere else, among men who are anxious for the independence of nations. But what effect will these events have upon the misunderstandings between us and the two great European powers? France, no one will suppose, is likely to lower her tone or change her decree; nor do I perceive any evidence of a disposition on the part of England, to recede from the ground she had taken. I do, notwithstanding, think that the repeal of the partial nonimportation law, the expiration of the law in virtue of which the English ships of war were excluded from our ports, and the late nonintercourse law, which is alike applicable to France and England, and which equally excludes the public and private ships of both, afford grounds for an overture on the part of England, which would very greatly embarrass our government. . . . But supposing the import of our last law to be known in England, and that it is actually believed that the President will exercise the power of suspending the law, in respect to either of the nations, which may recall their maritime decrees or orders, would it not be a wise step on the part of England, to offer to enter with us into a Convention, by which, in order to do away with existing and mutual embarrassments, and to re-establish the former friendship and harmonious intercourse between the two countries, it should be agreed and stipulated that England should recall her orders in Council so far as concerns the United States, and that the United States should repeal the law closing their ports against the public and private ships of England and imposing a nonintercourse and embargo, so far as respects England, and moreover stipulating that the law should be continued in force against France, until she shall repeal the maritime decrees? Should this overture be made, it would test the sincerity of our professions—and could not fail in creating the most serious difficulties in the Cabinet. It would however fail to restore harmony, because its restoration would inevitably be productive of an immediate war with France—and notwithstanding the President is by law authorized to replace things on their former footing on the repeal of the English orders, he would not dare to do so, because the dread of the influence of a French war upon the ruling party, is stronger and more controlling than the fear of shame, or the love of reputation. I at present discern no honorable course by which we are likely to be extricated from the embarrassments into which the folly of our own government has plunged the country. The new Congress will enter into the disgraceful controversies of the old; and I am apprehensive that nothing can or will be done by them, to rescue the nation from the ruinous condition of its affairs.

13. Thomas Baring Finds Prospects Gloomy in England, 4 October 1809.

The British government repudiated Erskine's Treaty, causing resentment in the United States and the prompt renewal of non-intercourse. The friends of America in England were as despondent as the friends of England in America. Foremost among the English friends of America were the Barings, who had long enriched themselves in the American trade and, like the Erskines, were connected by marriage to a distinguished Philadelphia family. By late 1809, they had about concluded that their efforts for reconciliation were useless. [*Life and Correspondence of Rufus King,* V, 171–72.]

. . . In our political speculation we must combine the general state of the world, which is almost divided into three parts, Europe, England and America, and which has introduced opinions and systems solely applicable to the present times. The last will only be considered by the two first, as she applies to their respective interests, when opposed to each other, and the questions of right and justice, and even solemn treaties, will vanish before those partial interests. The struggle is now for individual existence and unfortunately for us, those who govern are more hostile than favorable to commerce, imitating the conduct of France, and conceiving that peasants and soldiers alone contribute towards the physical strength of the country. Whilst those who reason on the subject with you, look at the minute details of the question, I fear that our Government will not yield to a full return of a free neutral trade, notwithstanding I am persuaded it is a benefit and not an injury to ourselves; at the same time I am equally satisfied that conciliation on our part would produce open hostilities from France, who has coquetted with America, since the disavowal of Erskine, and keeps the countries precisely in the situation in which she wishes us to remain. . . . The papers will inform you about a change of ministers; those who remain will have carried their point by the exclusion of the others, but the last letter from London announces a premier, who is distinguished for a narrow mind and tenacious disposition, unsupported by talent or character. It is however premature to pronounce on the 3rd of October. . . . Endeavors are used to alarm the public about the King's conscience, although without the slightest foundation, but it is easier to make John Bull swallow a lie, than truth, which is evident in the opinion generally entertained about our disputes with America by the public at large.

14. Henry Clay Advocates Arming for War, 31 December 1811.

In May, 1810, Congress replaced the Non-Intercourse Act with the oddly-named Macon's Bill No. 2, which lifted all commercial restrictions but promised to renew them against one belligerent should the other revoke its decrees and recognize American rights. Napoleon exploited this law by pretending to lift his blockades against American shipping. President Madison then reinstated the embargo against England and persisted in insisting, in his diplomacy, that Napoleon had respected American neutrality. As the diplomatic stalemate grew more ominous, the old problem of the Northwest flared again. In November, 1811, Indians fell upon a force of American troops under William Henry Harrison in the Indiana Territory. Although the British in Canada had actually

discouraged such dangerous attacks, they remained a poten-
tial ally and a continuous source of supply to the Indians, and
most citizens of the United States suspected much worse.
After years of commercial uncertainty, insults to our flag, and
self-denial in the hope of a peace that became ever more elu-
sive, President Madison recommended to his new Congress
in November, 1811, that it consider preparations for war.
Leadership in that Congress fell to a group of young men
willing to fight for the honor and prosperity of the United
States. One of these was Henry Clay of Kentucky; though
he was only thirty-four years old and a new member, the
House of Representatives elected him Speaker by a vote of
75 to 44. [*The Life and Speeches of Henry Clay* (New York,
1843), I, 15–21.]

. . . The first question which presents itself, in relation to this bill,
is as to the quantum of force which it proposes to raise. Is it too
large or too small—too strong or too weak? The contemplated army
is, to my mind, too great for peace; and I am fearful, far as it is above
the wishes of some of those with whom I generally have the honor
to act, that it is too small for the purposes of war. The bill provides
for the raising of twenty-five thousand troops; the bill recently
passed was intended to complete the enlistment for six thousand
more. The whole would amount to thirty-one thousand. Deducting
for sickness, to which raw troops are peculiarly exposed, and for
other deficiencies, a reasonable number of these troops, and to give
the most favorable result, we shall not raise by both bills more than
twenty or twenty-five thousand effective men. Could a country
boundless in extent, with a numerous line of forts and garrisons,
liable to invasions and predatory incursions at every point, be defended, and at the same time a war carried on, by a less number
of regulars than twenty-five thousand? If the legislative councils
err in such a case, they ought to err on the side of safety and vigor.
The question is—will you embark in a war which shall be feeble
and protracted to a great length of time, or will you make a vigorous
stroke and put an end to this territorial war at once? Canada is the
avowed object. Suppose you conquer Upper Canada, you must leave
men behind to hold it, when you march on Quebec. Your rear must
be protected; it would be a new mode of warfare to leave it un-

protected! Gentlemen will be deceived, if they calculate upon the treason of the Canadian people. Well, sir, you lay siege to Quebec, garrisoned, I am informed, by seven or eight thousand British forces; you must have at least double that number to take possession of the place. Suppose Quebec reduced; high as is my sense of the valor of my countrymen, I do not believe that militia or volunteers could be obtained to retain it for as long a period as would be necessary. But in respect to the question of economy, I conceive that it would be more expedient to raise a large force at once. With an army of twenty-five thousand men, the territorial war would probably terminate in one year; while it would last, waged with eight or ten thousand troops, three or four years. I said the territorial war; for it is probable that for years after the enemy shall be driven from the provinces, hostilities may be prosecuted on the ocean. So much for the quantum of the proposed force. Were I to amplify, as well I might; were I to draw too extensively on the patience of the Committee, they might feel disposed to protest my draft.

I advance to the consideration of the *nature* of the troops. Our republican jealousies, our love of liberty, the danger of standing armies, are themes which have been successfully touched, in discussing the subject before the Committee, at least so far as our feelings are concerned, however little weight they may have produced on our judgment. I do not stand on this floor as the advocate of standing armies in time of peace; but when war becomes essential, I *am* the advocate of raising able and vigorous armies to ensure its success. The danger of armies in peace arises from their idleness and dissipation; their corrupted habits, which mold them to the will of ambitious chieftains. We have been the subject of abuse for years by tourists through this country, whether on horseback or on foot, in prose or in poetry; but although we may not have exhibited as many great instances of discoveries and improvements in science, as the long established nations of Europe, the mass of our people possess more general political information than any people on earth; such information is universally diffused among us. This circumstance is one security against the ambition of military leaders. Another barrier is derived from the extent of the country, and the millions of people spread over its face. Paris was taken, and all France consequently subjugated. London might be subdued, and England would fall before the conqueror. But the population and strength of this country are concentrated in no one place. Philadelphia may be invaded; New York or Boston may fall; every seaport may be taken; but the country will remain free. The whole of our Territory on this side of the Allegheny may be invaded; still liberty will not be subdued. We have or will soon have eighteen state governments, capable and possessing the right to apply their immense pecuniary and physical military resources to oppose any daring usurper who may attempt to prostrate our liberties. The national government; one or more of the state sovereignties, may be annihilated; the country will yet be safe. We possess another security against the dangers of armies in the great body of militia. I hope to God that ere long we shall see every man proudly shoulder a musket to defend his liberties. Massachusetts at this time presents the noble spectacle of fifty or sixty thousand of her citizens with arms in their hands, ready to point their bayonets to the breast of any tyrant who may attempt to crush their freedom. And with all these securities, do gentlemen seriously apprehend danger from a pitiful army of 25 or 30,000 men? I trust not.

I must beg leave to differ with those gentlemen who have thought it improper to debate upon war in the face of day. It is impossible to conceal the measures of preparation for war. Have gentlemen ever known of a war between France and Russia, for example, without receiving accounts of its being meditated for weeks and months before it actually took place? You may pass your laws in secret, but you cannot secretly execute them. Men must be raised; can they be enlisted in the dark? I feel no difficulty on this point.

Gentlemen have inquired, what will be gained by the contemplated war? I ask, in turn, what will you not lose by your mongrel state of peace with Great Britain? Do you expect to gain anything in a pecuniary view? No, sir. Look at your treasury reports. We now receive only six millions of revenue annually; and this amount must be diminished in the same proportion as the rigorous execution of the orders in council shall increase. Before these orders existed we received sixteen millions. We lose, then, to the amount of ten millions of revenue per annum by our present peace. A war would probably produce the repeal of the orders in council; and our revenue would be restored; our commerce would flourish; our wealth and prosperity would advance. But certain gentlemen tell us to repeal the nonimportation, and then we shall have commerce and revenue. Admit that we could be guilty of so gross an act of perfidy, after we have voluntarily pledged our faith to that power which should revoke its hostile edicts, to enforce against its enemy this nonimportation; admit this; repeal your laws; and what will be the consequence? We shall present the strange phenomenon of an import without an export trade. We should become bankrupt, if we should thus carry on a trade. Where would our produce find vent? Under the British orders, we cannot send it to the markets of continental Europe. Will Great Britain take our exports? She has no market for them; her people can find use for only a small portion of them. By a continuance of this peace, then, we shall lose our commerce, our character, and a nation's best attribute, our honor. A war will give us commerce and character; and we shall enjoy the proud consciousness of having discharged our highest duty to our country.

But England, it seems, is fighting the battles of mankind; and we are asked, shall we weaken her magnanimous efforts? For argument's sake, let us concede the fact, that the French Emperor is aiming at universal empire; can Great Britain challenge our sympathies, when, instead of putting forth her arms to protect the world, she has converted the war into a means of self-aggrandizement; when, under pretense of defending them, she has destroyed the commerce and trampled on the rights of every nation; when she has attempted to annihilate every vestige of the public maritime code of which she professes to be the champion? Shall we swallow the potion of British poison, lest we may be presented with the imperial dose? Are we called upon to bow to the mandates of royal insolence, as a preparation to contend against Gallic usurpation? Who ever learned in the school of base submission, the lessons of noble freedom, and courage, and independence? Look at Spain. Did she secure her independence by submitting, in the first instance, to the dictates of imperial usurpations? No, sir. If she had resisted the first intrusion into her councils, her monarch would not at this time be a miserable victim in the dungeons of Marseilles. We cannot secure our independence of one power, by a dastardly submission to the will of another. But look at our own history. Our ancestors of the Revolution resisted the first encroachments of British tyranny. They foresaw that by submitting to pay an illegal tax, contemptible as that was in itself, their liberties would ultimately be subverted. Consider the progress of the present disputes with England. For what were we contending the other day? For the indirect colonial carrying trade. That has vanished. For what are we now deliberating? For the direct export and import trade; the trade in our own cotton, and tobacco, and fish. Give this up, and tomorrow we must take up arms for our right to pass from New York to New Orleans; from the upper country on James River to Richmond. Sir, when did submission to one wrong induce an adversary to cease his encroachments on the party submitting? But we are told that we ought only to go to war when our territory is invaded. How much better than invasion is the blocking of our very ports and harbors; insulting our towns; plundering our merchants, and scouring our coasts? If our fields are surrounded, are they in a better condition than if invaded? When the murderer is at our doors, shall we meanly skulk to our cells? Or shall we boldly oppose him at his entrance?

I could wish the past were buried in oblivion. But we cannot shut our eyes. The other day, the pretense for the orders in council was retaliation for the French edicts. The existence of these edicts was made the ground of Sir William Scott, for the condemnation of the *Fox* and others. It will be recollected that Sir William had delayed his sentence in the celebrated case, that proof of the repeal of the French decrees might be produced. They were produced. Nevertheless the condemnation took place. But the plea of retaliation has given way to other pretexts and other claims. To the astonishment of all mankind, the British envoy has demanded as a preliminary to the revocation of the orders in council, that the United States shall cause the continental ports to be opened for the admission of British manufactures! We are required to compel France to repeal her *municipal code* itself! Sir, these are some of the motives of the British hostility to our commerce. She sickens at our prosperity; she is jealous of us; she dreads our rivalship on the ocean. If you doubt this, look at our trade in 1806. Our trade with England was twelve or thirteen millions in her favor. We bought fifty millions worth of her manufactures. We furnished her with the necessaries of life, and in exchange, accepted her luxuries. How was our trade with France and Holland? Our exports to both these countries amounted to eighteen millions, our imports to twenty-five millions. Considering the superiority in trade with us, which Great Britain enjoyed over her rival, would she have relinquished that superiority, would she have given up her profitable trade, for the single purpose of humbling that of her antagonist? Would she have hazarded the evils of a war with this country for this object? No, sir, she sees in our numberless ships, whose sails spread upon every sea; she perceives in our hundred and twenty thousand gallant tars, the seeds of a naval force, which in thirty years, will rival her on her own element. She therefore commences the odious system of impressment, of which no language can paint my indignant execration; she dares to attempt the subversion of the personal freedom of our mariners. She aims at depressing our commerce, which she foresees will induce our seamen to enter her service, will impair the means of cherishing our navy, of protecting and extending our commerce, and will at the same time raise her own power.

Sir, we are told this government is not calculated to stand the shock of war; that gentlemen will lose their seats in this and the other House; that our benches will be filled by other men, who after we have carried on the war, will make for us an ignominious peace. I cannot believe that to retain their seats is the extent of the *amor patriae* of gentlemen in this House. Can we let our brave countrymen, a Daviess and his associates in arms, perish in manfully fighting our battles, while we meanly cling to our places? But I cannot persuade myself that the nation will be ungrateful. I am convinced that when they know that their government has been strictly impartial towards the belligerents—for surely no gentleman in this House can be so base as to ascribe partiality or other improper motives to us—when they perceive the sincere and persevering exertions of their government to preserve peace; they will continue to adhere to it, even in an unsuccessful war to defend their rights, to assert their honor, the dignity and independence of the country. But my ideas of duty are such, that when my rights are invaded, I must advance to their defense, let what may be the consequence; even if death itself were to be my certain fate.

I must apologize for having trespassed so long upon the patience of the Committee. I trust that I have fully established these three positions: that the quantum of the force proposed by the bill is not too great—that its nature is such as the contemplated war calls for; and that the object of the war is justified by every consideration of justice, of interest, of honor, and love of country. Unless the object is attained by peaceful means, I hope that war will be waged before the close of the session.

15. Congress Receives the Henry Letters, 9 March 1812.

Even in the spring of 1812, James Madison still hoped for a diplomatic solution to the impasse with Britain. The growing belligerence of Congress might frighten the British government, which scarcely could afford an American war. But Madison needed, for maximum diplomatic success, more convincing proof that Bonaparte had repealed his decrees. In fact he had not done so, and everyone knew it. Although only pretended proof was forthcoming—a predated and spurious document known as the Decree of St. Cloud—Madison made the most of it. More useful to him was John Henry, the turncoat British spy who, as agent of the governor of Canada had investigated pro-British sentiment in New England in 1809. Incensed at what he considered insufficient pay for his services, Henry undertook to sell copies of his intelligence reports to the United States government, which agreed to pay $50,000 for them. The papers failed to silence the Federalists, for their contents were familiar enough. Their publication, attended by partisan recriminations against England and the friends of England in the United States, certainly contributed to the coming of war. The papers were put before Congress as if Henry had freely given them to the United States. Reproduced below are excerpts from President Madison's covering message, from Henry's pretended letter of gift, and from the sixth and seventh of his fifteen letters. [Benton, *Abridgement of the Debates of Congress* (New York, 1857), IV, 506, 509–10.]

To the Senate and House of Representatives of the United States:

I lay before Congress copies of certain documents which remain in the Department of State. They prove that at a recent period, whilst the United States, notwithstanding the wrongs sustained by them, ceased not to observe the laws of peace and neutrality towards Great Britain, and in the midst of amicable professions and negotiations on the part of the British Government, through its public ministers here, a secret agent of that Government was employed in certain States, more especially at the seat of Government in Massachusetts, in fomenting disaffection to the constituted authorities of the nation; and in intrigues with the disaffected for the purpose of bringing about resistance to the laws; and eventually, in concert with a British force, of destroying the Union and forming the Eastern part thereof into a political connection with Great Britain.

In addition to the effect which the discovery of such a procedure ought to have on the public councils, it will not fail to render more dear to the hearts of all good citizens that happy Union of these states, which, under Divine Providence, is the guarantee of their liberties, their safety, their tranquility, and their prosperity.

James Madison

To Hon. James Monroe, Secretary of State
Sir: Much observation and experience have convinced me, that the injuries and insults with which the United States have been so long and so frequently visited, and which cause their present embarrassment, have been owing to an opinion entertained by foreign states, "that in any measure tending to wound their pride, or provoke their hostility, the Government of this country could never induce a great majority of its citizens to concur." And as many of the evils which flow from the influence of this opinion on the policy of foreign nations, may be removed by any act that can produce unanimity among all parties in America, I voluntarily tender to you sir, such means, as I possess, towards promoting so desirable and important an object; which, if accomplished, cannot fail to extinguish, perhaps forever, those expectations abroad, which may protract indefinitely

an accommodation of existing differences, and check the progress of industry and prosperity in this rising Empire.

I have the honor to transmit herewith the documents and correspondence relating to an important mission in which I was employed by Sir James Craig, the late Governor General of the British Provinces in North America, in the winter of the year 1809.

The publication of these papers will demonstrate a fact not less valuable than the good already proposed; it will prove that no reliance ought to be placed on the professions of good faith of an Administration, which, by a series of disastrous events, has fallen into such hands as a Castlereagh, a Wellesley, or a Liverpool—I should rather say into the hands of the stupid subalterns, to whom the pleasures and the indolence of those ministers have consigned it.

In contributing to the good of the United States by an exposition which cannot (I think) fail to solve and melt all division and disunion among its citizens, I flatter myself with the fond expectation that when it is made public in England it will add one great motive to the many that already exist, to induce that nation to withdraw its confidence from men whose political career is a fruitful source of injury and embarrassment in America; of injustice and misery in Ireland; of distress and apprehension in England; and contempt everywhere . . .

J. Henry

To His Excellency the Governor-General, etc.
No. 6   Boston, March 5, 1809
Sir: I am favored with another opportunity of writing to you by a private conveyance; and think it probable, at this season, that the frequency of these will render it unnecessary to write to you in cipher.

It does not yet appear necessary that I should discover to any person the purpose of my visit to Boston; nor is it probable that I shall be compelled, for the sake of gaining more knowledge of the arrangements of the Federal party in these States, to avow myself as a regular authorized agent of the British Government, even to those individuals who would feel equally bound with myself to preserve, with the utmost inscrutability, so important a secret from the public eye. I have sufficient means of information to enable me to judge of the proper period for offering the co-operation of Great Britain, and opening a correspondence between the Governor General of British America, and those individuals who, from the part they take in the opposition to the National Government, or the influence they may possess in any new order of things that may grow out of the present differences, should be qualified to act on behalf of the Northern States. An apprehension of any such state of things as is presupposed by these remarks begins to subside, since it has appeared, by the conduct of the General Government, that it is seriously alarmed at the menacing attitude of the Northern States. But, although it is believed that there is no probability of an immediate war, yet no doubts are entertained that Mr. Madison will fall upon some new expedient to bring about hostilities. What these may be, can only be deduced from what appears to be practicable. A *nonintercourse* with England and France will probably supersede the embargo; which, by opening with the rest of Europe a partial, legitimate commerce, and offering strong temptations to that which is illegal, will expose the vessels to capture, detention, and embarrassment; will justify the present policy, and produce such a degree of irritation and resentment as will enable the Government of this country to throw the whole blame and responsibility of war from its own shoulders upon those of the British Ministry. If, in this, the party attached to France should calculate with correctness, and the commerce of New England should greatly suffer, the merchants, being injured and discouraged, would not only acquiesce in the restrictive system, but even submit to war. On the other hand, should the small traffic, permitted by a non-intercourse law, be lucrative and uninterrupted, the people would be clamorous for more, and soon compel the Government to restore the friendly relations between the two countries. . . .

No. 7 (In cipher)   Boston, March 7, 1809.
Sir: I have now ascertained, with as much accuracy as possible, the course intended to be pursued by the party in Massachusetts that is opposed to the measures and politics of the Administration of the General Government.

I have already given a decided opinion that a declaration of war is not to be expected; but, contrary to all reasonable calculation, should the Congress possess spirit and independence enough to place their popularity in jeopardy by so strong a measure, the Legislature of Massachusetts will give the tone to the neighboring States, will declare itself permanent until a new election of members, invite a Congress, to be composed of delegates from the Federal States, and erect a separate government for their common defense and common interest. This Congress would probably begin by abrogating the offensive laws, and adopting a plan for the maintenance of the power and authority thus assumed. They would, by such an act, be in a condition to make or receive proposals from Great Britain; and I should seize the first moment to open a correspondence with your Excellency. Scarcely any other aid would be necessary, and perhaps none required, than a few vessels of war from the Halifax station, to protect the maritime towns from the little navy which is at the disposal of the National Government. What permanent connection between Great Britain and this section of the Republic would grow out of a civil commotion, such as might be expected, no person is prepared to describe; but it seems that a strict alliance must result of necessity. At present the opposition party confine their calculations merely to resistance; and I can assure you that, at this moment, they do not freely entertain the project of withdrawing the Eastern States from the Union, finding it a very unpopular topic; although a course of events, such as I have already mentioned, would inevitably produce an incurable alienation of the New England from the Southern States.

The truth is, the common people have so long regarded the Constitution of the United States with complacency, that they are now only disposed in this quarter to treat it like a truant mistress, whom they would, for a time, put away on a separate maintenance, but, without further and greater provocation, would not absolutely repudiate. . . .

16. President Madison's War Message, 1 June 1812.

James Madison was a dedicated and intelligent patriot. He had wide learning and a subtle mind. By training and temperament, he was a scholarly politician and a moralist. Although he had the best of intentions, he was not a military leader. The diplomacy and politics of his first administration had been aimed at proving to the British that they were in the wrong and that, being in the wrong, they must suffer unless they mended their ways. Madison's War Message is a triumphant summary of the moral superiority of the American position as he had developed it for many years. But whereas it scolded the British, it did not menace them, for Madison had not yet built the army that Congress had only recently authorized, and such was the force of old Republican principles that Congress still would not authorize an increase in the Navy.

Perhaps even at this advanced date, Madison was trying, merely by threatening it, to avoid having war become a reality. Like the New England Federalists, he believed Napoleon both secure and formidable in Europe. But whereas the Federalists would use this belief as a ground for meeting Britain more than halfway, Madison would calculate that the British, pinned down by Napoleon, could not afford a war with the United States and must immediately treat on terms favorable to us. [Hunt, *Writings of James Madison* (New York, 1908), VIII, 192–94, 198–200.]

To the Senate and House of Representatives of the United States:

I communicate to Congress certain documents, being a continuation of those heretofore laid before them on the subject of our affairs with Great Britain.

Without going back beyond the renewal in 1803 of the war in which Great Britain is engaged, and omitting unrepaired wrongs of inferior magnitude, the conduct of her Government presents a series of acts hostile to the United States as an independent and neutral nation.

British cruisers have been in the continued practice of violating the American flag on the great highway of nations, and of seizing and carrying off persons sailing under it, not in the exercise of a belligerent right founded on the law of nations against an enemy, but of a municipal prerogative over British subjects. British jurisdiction is thus extended to neutral vessels in a situation where no laws can operate but the law of nations and the laws of the country to which the vessels belong, and a self-redress is assumed which, if British subjects were wrongfully detained and alone concerned, is that substitution of force for a resort to the responsible sovereign which falls within the definition of war. Could the seizure of British subjects in such cases be regarded as within the exercise of a belligerent right, the acknowledged laws of war, which forbid an article of captured property to be adjudged without a regular investigation before a competent tribunal, would imperiously demand the fairest trial where the sacred rights of persons were at issue. In place of such a trial these rights are subjected to the will of every petty commander.

The practice, hence, is so far from affecting British subjects alone, that, under the pretext of searching for these, thousands of American citizens, under the safeguard of public law and of their national flag, have been torn from their country and from everything dear to them; have been dragged on board ships of war of a foreign nation and exposed, under the severities of their discipline, to be exiled to the most distant and deadly climes, to risk their lives in the battles of their oppressors, and to be the melancholy instruments of taking away those of their own brethren.

Against this crying enormity, which Great Britain would be so prompt to avenge if committed against herself, the United States have in vain exhausted remonstrances and expostulations, and that no proof might be wanting of their conciliatory dispositions, and no pretext left for a continuance of the practice, the British Government was formally assured of the readiness of the United States to enter into arrangements such as could not be rejected if the recovery of British subjects were the real and the sole object. The communication passed without effect.

British cruisers have been in the practice also of violating the rights and the peace of our coasts. They hover over and harass our entering and departing commerce. To the most insulting pretensions they have added the most lawless proceedings in our very harbors, and have wantonly spilt American blood within the sanctuary of our territorial jurisdiction. The principles and rules enforced by that nation, when a neutral nation, against armed vessels of belligerents hovering near her coasts and disturbing her commerce are well known. When called on, nevertheless, by the United States to punish the greater offenses committed by her own vessels, her Government has bestowed on their commanders additional marks of honor and confidence.

Under pretended blockades, without the presence of an adequate force and sometimes without the practicability of applying one, our commerce has been plundered in every sea, the great staples of our country have been cut off from their legitimate markets, and a destructive blow aimed at our agricultural and maritime interests. In aggravation of these predatory measures they have been considered as in force from the dates of their notification, a retrospective effect being thus added, as has been done in other important cases, to the unlawfulness of the course pursued. And to render the outrage the more signal these mock blockades have been reiterated and enforced in the face of official communications from the British Government declaring as the true definition of a legal blockade "that particular ports must be actually invested and previous warning given to vessels bound to them not to enter."

Not content with these occasional expedients for laying waste our neutral trade, the cabinet of Britain resorted at length to the sweeping system of blockades, under the name of orders in council, which has been molded and managed as might best suit its political views, its commercial jealousies, or the avidity of British cruisers. . . .

There was a period when a favorable change in the policy of the British cabinet was justly considered as established. The minister plenipotentiary of His Britannic Majesty here proposed an adjustment of the differences more immediately endangering the harmony of the two countries. The proposition was accepted with the promptitude and cordiality corresponding with the invariable professions of this Government. A foundation appeared to be laid for a sincere and lasting reconciliation. The prospect, however, quickly vanished. The whole proceeding was disavowed by the British Government without any explanations which could at that time repress the belief that the disavowal proceeded from a spirit of hostility to the commercial rights and prosperity of the United States; and it has since come into proof that at the very moment when the public minister was holding the language of friendship and inspiring confidence in the sincerity of the negotiation with which he was charged a secret agent of his Government was employed in intrigues having for their object a subversion of our Government and a dismemberment of our happy union.

In reviewing the conduct of Great Britian toward the United States our attention is necessarily drawn to the warfare just renewed by the savages on one of our extensive frontiers—a warfare which is known to spare neither age nor sex and to be distinguished by features peculiarly shocking to humanity. It is difficult to account for the activity and combinations which have for some time been developing themselves among tribes in constant intercourse with British traders and garrisons without connecting their hostility with that influence and without recollecting the authenticated examples of such interpositions heretofore furnished by the officers and agents of that Government. . . .

We behold, in fine, on the side of Great Britain, a state of war against the United States, and on the side of the United States a state of peace toward Great Britain. Whether the United States shall continue passive under these progressive usurpations and these accumulating wrongs, or, opposing force to force in defense of their national rights, shall commit a just cause into the hands of the Almighty Disposer of Events, avoiding all connections which might entangle it in the contest or views of other powers, and preserving a constant readiness to concur in an honorable re-establishment of peace and friendship, is a solemn question which the Constitution wisely confides to the legislative department of the Government. In recommending it to their early deliberations I am happy in the assurance that the decision will be worthy the enlightened and patriotic councils of a virtuous, a free, and a powerful nation.

* * *

17. Gouverneur Morris on Monroe's Strategy and "Federal Gudgeons," 1 November 1814.

In 1790, Gouverneur Morris had been a firm supporter of the alliance with France and of a tough line with Britain, but the progress of the French Revolution had reversed his politics. As an old man settled on his grand estate of Morrisania, he encouraged Timothy Pickering and others to form a regional convention, which finally met in Hartford on 15 December. This was to become the denouement of that political impulse, once so formidable and effective under the leadership of Alexander Hamilton, toward the belief that the best future for America would be in a sort of partnership with the British Empire. With Napoleon apparently crushed, the British had attacked the United States severely and on several fronts in 1814, not failing to raid and invade New England. While Federalists could find ample evidence of bad management in Madison's war leadership, the logic and wisdom of the Hartford protests—so far as they were logical and wise—were lost in the rebirth of patriotism. The public had no time for the legalisms of Hartford, except to execrate them as traitorous. The following letter shows the degree to which Morris had lost touch with popular feeling. This was a time of celebration of Macdonough's triumph at Plattsburgh and of the defeat of the British at Fort McHenry, as well as a time of preparation for the next assault. But Morris placed his hope in the forthcoming Hartford Convention. [Morris to Pickering, in Lodge, *Life and Letters of George Cabot,* pp. 537–38.]

Dear Sir,

I have received yours of the 21st of October, and now see that we are to be taxed beyond our means, and subjected to military conscription. These measures are devised and pursued by the gentle spirits who for more than twenty years have lavished on Britain the bitterest vulgarity of Billingsgate, because she impressed her seamen for self-defense, and have shed a torrent of crocodile tears over the poor of that country, crushed, as they pretend, by oppressive taxes to gratify royal ambition. Nevertheless, this waste of men and money, neither of which can be squeezed out of our extenuated States, is proposed for the conquest of Canada. And thus after swearing and forswearing backward and forward till their fondest adherents were grown giddy, and after publishing their willingness to abandon every former pretext, the administration boldly avow that, although we are so simple as to call this a war of defense, it is still on their part a war of conquest.

What will the Federal gentlemen now say, who, to excuse their support of this administration, assumed that their unprovoked, unwise, unjust war of aggression had, all at once, become defensive. I admire and applaud the proud consistency of our adversaries, who say to these over-quondam friends: "We disdain your proffered support. You shall not participate in power, neither shall your quibble serve your turn. We wage no defensive war, but mean to conquer Canada. Vote for that or vote against us, we care not which."

And now, my good friend, be, I pray you, so kind as to tell the pliant patriots who become converts to Mr. Monroe's scheme, frankly communicated to enemies as to friends, of marching into Canada by way of inducing the British forces on our coast to meet us there, that, the St. Lawrence being no longer navigable, this sublime diversion cannot take effect before the month of May. But perhaps the Secretary, as facetious as he is sagacious, meant this diversion merely as a pleasantry to divert himself and his colleagues at the eagerness with which Federal gudgeons will, in the lack of bait, swallow a bare hook.

Doubts are, I find, entertained whether Massachusetts is in earnest, and whether she will be supported by the New England family. But surely these outrageous measures must rouse their patriot sentiment to cast off the load of oppression.

18. A Proper Conclusion: Thomas Jefferson to the Marquis de Lafayette, 14 February 1815.

Under the leadership of the War Hawks and under the force of circumstances, the Democratic-Republicans adopted during the War of 1812 the leading principles of Washingtonian Federalism. At the end of the war, they were prepared to foster industries, charter a national bank, maintain and enlarge the Navy, and improve internal communications. Though young men like Clay and John C. Calhoun took the lead in Congress, many older men approved of their program, among them the aging but still astute Jefferson. As a further sign of Jefferson's flexibility, compare his reflections on the

French Revolution composed in 1815 with those of 1793
(Part I, No. 8). Jefferson reached in 1815 the view that
Morris and Hamilton had held in 1792! [Ford, *Writings of
Jefferson*, IX, 505–6, 508, 510.]

. . . Possibly you may remember, at the date of the *jeu de paume*,
how earnestly I urged yourself and the patriots of my acquaintance,
to enter then into a compact with the king, securing freedom of religion, freedom of the press, trial by jury, *habeas corpus*, and a national legislature, all of which it was known he would then yield; to
go home, and let these work on the amelioration of the condition of
the people, until they should have rendered them capable of more,
when occasions would not fail to arise for communicating to them
more. This was as much as I then thought them able to bear, soberly
and usefully for themselves. You thought otherwise, and that the
dose might still be larger. And I found you were right; for subsequent events proved they were equal to the constitution of 1791. Unfortunately, some of the most honest and enlightened of our patriotic
friends, (but closet politicians merely, unpracticed in the knowledge of man,) thought more could still be obtained and borne. They
did not weigh the hazards of a transition from one form of government to another, the value of what they had already rescued from
those hazards, and might hold in security if they pleased, nor the
imprudence of giving up the certainty of such a degree of liberty,
under a limited monarch, for the uncertainty of a little more under
the form of a republic.

You differed from them. You were for stopping there, and for
securing the constitution which the National Assembly had obtained. Here, too, you were right; and from this fatal error of the
republicans, from their separation from yourself and the constitu-
tionalists, in their councils, flowed all the subsequent sufferings and
crimes of the French nation. The hazards of a second change fell
upon them by the way. The foreigner gained time to anarchise by
gold the government he could not overthrow by arms, to crush in
their own councils the genuine republicans, by the fraternal em-
braces of exaggerated and hired pretenders, and to turn the machine
of Jacobinism from the change to the destruction of order; and, in
the end, the limited monarchy they had secured was exchanged for

the unprincipled and bloody tyranny of Robespierre, and the equally unprincipled and maniac tyranny of Bonaparte. . . .

The British have hoped more in their Hartford Convention. Their fears of republican France being now done away, they are directed to republican America, and they are playing the same game for disorganization here, which they played in your country. The Marats, the Dantons, and Robespierres of Massachusetts are in the same pay, under the same orders, and making the same efforts to anarchise us, that their prototypes in France did there.

I do not say that all who met at Hartford were under the same motives of money, nor were those of France. Some of them are Outs, and wish to be Ins; some the mere dupes of agitators, or of their own party passions, while the Maratists alone are in the real secret; but they have very different materials to work on. The yeomanry of the United States are not the *canaille* of Paris. We might safely give them leave to go through the United States recruiting their ranks, and I am satisfied they could not raise one single regiment (gambling merchants and silk-stocking clerks excepted) who would support them in any effort to separate from the Union. The cement of this Union is in the heartblood of every American. I do not believe there is on earth a government established on so immovable a basis. Let them, in any state, even in Massachusetts itself, raise the standard of separation, and its citizens will rise in mass, and do justice themselves on their own incendiaries. If they could have induced the government to some effort of suppression, or even to enter into discussion with them, it would have given them some importance, have brought them some notice. But they have not been able to make themselves even a subject of conversation, either of public or private societies. A silent contempt has been the sole notice they excite. . . .

P. S. February 26th. My letter had not yet been sealed, when I received news of our peace. I am glad of it, and especially that we closed our war with the *éclat* of the action at New Orleans. But I consider it as an armistice only, because no security is provided against the impressment of our seamen. While this is unsettled we are in hostility of mind with England, although actual deeds of arms may be suspended by a truce. If she thinks the exercise of this outrage is worth eternal war, eternal war it must be, or extermination of the one or the other party. The first act of impressment she commits on an American, will be answered by reprisal, or by a declaration of war here; and the interval must be merely a state of preparation for it. In this we have much to do, in further fortifying our seaport towns, providing military stores, classing and disciplining our militia, arranging our financial system, and above all, pushing our domestic manufactures, which have taken such root as never again can be shaken. Once more, God bless you.

Suggestions for Further Reading

There is a fascinating interpretation of early United States foreign policy in William A. Williams, *The Contours of American History* (Cleveland, 1961). For an equally stimulating and more detailed study of the subject, see Paul A. Varg, *The Foreign Policies of the Founding Fathers* (East Lansing, 1963). A brief and lucid introduction to the subject is Felix Gilbert, *To the Farewell Address: Ideas of Early American Foreign Policy* (Princeton, 1961).

For the intimate relationship between foreign issues and domestic politics, four large-scale biographies are unusually valuable. (1) Dumas Malone, *Jefferson and His Time:* Vol. II, *Jefferson and the Rights of Man,* and Vol. III, *Jefferson and the Ordeal of Liberty* (Boston, 1951 and 1962). (2) Irving Brant, *James Madison* (Indianapolis and New York, 1941–1961), in six volumes, the last four of which cover Madison's long career as a national leader under the Constitution. (3) Douglas Southall Freeman, *George Washington:* Vol. VI, *Patriot and President,* and Vol. VII (by John Alexander Carroll and Mary Wells Ashworth), *First in Peace* (New York, 1953–57). (4) Samuel Flagg Bemis, *John Quincy Adams and the Foundations of American Foreign Policy* (New York, 1949).

Another biography should be mentioned for its full and fair discussion of New England Federalism during the years of international crisis: Samuel Eliot Morison, *The Life and Letters of Harrison Gray Otis.* 2 vols. (Boston and New York, 1913). Weak in analysis, but valuable for quantities of material from the popular press and the debates of Congress, is John Bach McMaster, *A History of the People of the United States,* Vols.

175

II–IV (New York and London, 1914). Henry Adams gave far more attention to foreign affairs than to any other subject in his nine-volume *History of the United States in the Administrations of Jefferson and Madison*, which is available in several editions, including abridgements. Robert R. Palmer's *The Age of the Democratic Revolution*, Vol. II: *The Struggle* (Princeton, 1964), takes a wider view of politics and diplomacy than we usually are treated to. Charles A. Beard, *The Economic Origins of Jeffersonian Democracy* (New York, 1915) still remains the most ambitious attempt to understand the material interests underlying the early politics of the nation.

Relations between the United States and Spain are the subject of several fine monographs. Arthur Preston Whitaker has written three: *The Spanish-American Frontier, 1783–1795* (Boston and New York, 1927), *The Mississippi Question* (New York and London, 1934), and *The United States and the Independence of Latin America* (Baltimore, 1941). To these should be added S. F. Bemis, *Pinckney's Treaty*, revised edition (New Haven, 1960). The diplomatic relations of the United States with France are carefully unfolded by Alexander DeConde in *Entangling Alliance* (Durham, 1958) and *The Quasi-War* (New York, 1966).

The relations of the United States with Great Britain naturally have received the most exhaustive scholarly attention. An authoritative survey is A. L. Burt, *The United States, Great Britain, and British North America, from the Revolution to the Establishment of Peace after the War of 1812* (New Haven, Toronto, and London, 1940). More specialized treatments may be found in S. F. Bemis, *Jay's Treaty*, revised edition (New Haven, 1962) and in three volumes by Bradford Perkins: *The First Rapprochement* (Philadelphia, 1955), *Prologue to War* (Berkeley and Los Angeles, 1963), and *Castlereagh and Adams* (Berkeley and Los Angeles, 1964). To these should be added the sensible book by Reginald Horsman, *The Causes of the War of 1812* (Philadelphia, 1962).

Most of the books listed above have a full complement of notes and bibliographical references. They will serve as guides to the immense resources of newspapers, pamphlets, collections of private and public papers, and scholarly works that tell us about early United States history.